SLOW COOKING RECIPES 2022

TASTY RECIPES EASY TO MAKE FOR BEGINNERS

JAMES SINS

Table of Contents

Geoff's Easy Roast Chicken with Gravy 21

INGREDIENTS 21

PREPARATION 21

Gingered Pineapple Chicken 22

INGREDIENTS 22

PREPARATION 22

Greek Chicken 23

INGREDIENTS 23

PREPARATION 24

Hawaiian Drumsticks 25

INGREDIENTS 25

PREPARATION 25

Herbed Chicken With Vegetables 26

INGREDIENTS 26

PREPARATION 27

Herbed Chicken with Wild Rice 28

INGREDIENTS 28

PREPARATION 29

Honey and Ginger Chicken 30

INGREDIENTS 30

PREPARATION 31

Honey Barbecued Chicken with Sweet Potatoes 32

INGREDIENTS 32

PREPARATION 33

Honey Hoisin Chicken 34

INGREDIENTS 34

PREPARATION 35

Italian Style Chicken 36

INGREDIENTS 36

PREPARATION 37

Italian Style Chicken in the Crockpot 38

INGREDIENTS 38

PREPARATION 39

Italian Style Chicken With Spaghetti, Slow Cooker 40

INGREDIENTS 40

PREPARATION 41

Light Chicken Stroganoff 42

INGREDIENTS 42

PREPARATION 43

Lilly's Slow Cooker Chicken With Cheese Sauce 44

INGREDIENTS 44

PREPARATION 44

Mexican-Style Chicken Breasts 45

INGREDIENTS 45

- Optional Garnishes 46

PREPARATION 46

Paula's Chicken With Leeks 48

INGREDIENTS 48

PREPARATION 48

Saucy Jack Daniel's Barbecue Chicken Drumettes 49

INGREDIENTS 49

- Barbecue Sauce 49

PREPARATION 51

Sherri's Chicken & Dumplings 52

INGREDIENTS 52

PREPARATION 53

Simple Slow Cooker Chicken Barbecue 54

INGREDIENTS 54

PREPARATION 54

Slow-Cooked Chicken Dijon 55

INGREDIENTS 55

PREPARATION 55

Slow Cooker Barbecue Chicken 56

INGREDIENTS 56

PREPARATION 56

Slow Cooker Barbecued Chicken Thighs 57

INGREDIENTS 57

PREPARATION 57

Slow Cooker Chicken and Sausage Pasta Sauce 58

INGREDIENTS 58

PREPARATION 59

Slow Cooker Chicken Curry 60

INGREDIENTS 60

PREPARATION 60

Slow Cooker Chicken Curry With Rice 61

INGREDIENTS 61

PREPARATION 62

Slow Cooker Chicken Enchiladas 63

INGREDIENTS 63

PREPARATION 64

Slow Cooker Chicken Fricassee With Vegetables 65

INGREDIENTS 65

PREPARATION 66

Slow Cooker Chicken in Spicy Sauce 67

INGREDIENTS 67

PREPARATION 67

Slow Cooker Chicken Madras With Curry Powder 68

INGREDIENTS 68

PREPARATION 68

Slow Cooker Chicken With Mushrooms 69

INGREDIENTS 69

PREPARATION 70

Slow Cooker Cordon Bleu 71

INGREDIENTS 71

PREPARATION 72

Slow Cooker Dijon Chicken 73

INGREDIENTS 73

PREPARATION 73

Slow Cooker Lemon Chicken 75

INGREDIENTS 75

PREPARATION 76

Slow Cooker Pulled Chicken 77

INGREDIENTS 77

PREPARATION 78

Smoked Sausage and Cabbage 79

INGREDIENTS 79

PREPARATION 80

Spanish Chicken With Rice 81

INGREDIENTS 81

PREPARATION 82

Tami's Barbecued Chicken Legs 83

INGREDIENTS 83

PREPARATION 83

Tami's Crockpot Chicken Mozzarella... 84

INGREDIENTS 84

PREPARATION 84

White Chicken Chili 85

INGREDIENTS 85

PREPARATION 85

Slow Cooker Chicken and Black Beans...................................... 86

INGREDIENTS 86

PREPARATION 87

Chicken and Dressing, Slow Cooker 88

INGREDIENTS 88

PREPARATION 88

Chicken and Mushrooms, Slow Cooker 89

INGREDIENTS 89

PREPARATION 90

Chicken and Rice Parmesan, Slow Cooker 91

INGREDIENTS 91

PREPARATION 91

Chicken and Shrimp 92

INGREDIENTS 92

PREPARATION 93

Chicken and Stuffing Recipe 94

INGREDIENTS 94

PREPARATION 94

Chicken Breasts in Creamy Creole Sauce 96

INGREDIENTS 96

PREPARATION 97

Chicken Chili with Hominy 98

INGREDIENTS 98

PREPARATION 98

Chicken Delish 99

INGREDIENTS 99

PREPARATION 100

Chicken Enchiladas for the Slow Cooker 101

INGREDIENTS 101

PREPARATION 101

Chicken Las Vegas 102

INGREDIENTS 102

PREPARATION 102

Chicken Parisienne for the Slow Cooker 103

INGREDIENTS 103

PREPARATION 103

Chicken Reuben Casserole, Slow Cooker 104

INGREDIENTS 104

PREPARATION 104

Chicken with Cranberries 105

INGREDIENTS 105

PREPARATION 105

Chicken with Dressing and Gravy, Slow Cooker 106

INGREDIENTS 106

PREPARATION 107

Chicken with Macaroni and Smoked Gouda Cheese 108

INGREDIENTS 108

PREPARATION 109

Chicken With Pearl Onions and Mushrooms, Slow Cooker 110

INGREDIENTS 110

PREPARATION 110

Chicken With Pineapple 111

INGREDIENTS 111

PREPARATION 112

Country Captain Chicken 113

INGREDIENTS 113

PREPARATION 114

Country Chicken and Mushrooms 115

INGREDIENTS 115

PREPARATION 115

Cranberry Chicken 116

INGREDIENTS 116

PREPARATION 117

Creamy Italian Chicken 118

INGREDIENTS 118

PREPARATION 118

Crockpot Korean Short Rib Tacos 119

Ingredients	119
Instructions	120
For the Ribs	120
For the Slaw	121
Provencal Chicken and Beans	123
Ingredients	123
Directions	123
Buffalo Chicken Sandwiches (Made in the Crockpot)	124
Directions	124
Slow Cooker Spicy Barbecued Chicken	125
Ingredients	125
Directions	126
Slow Cooker Salsa Chicken	128
Ingredients	128
Directions	128
Pulled Pork with Caramelized Onions	129
Ingredients	129
Directions	130
Slow Cooker Marinara Chicken and Vegetables	131
Ingredients	131
Directions	132

Slow Cooker Lemon Chicken 133

Ingredients 133

Directions 134

Vegetarian Chili Ole! Recipe 135

Ingredients 135

Directions 136

Char Siu Pork Roast 137

Ingredients 137

Preparation 138

Thyme-Scented White Bean Cassoulet 139

Ingredients 139

Preparation 140

Vegetable and Chickpea Curry 141

Ingredients 141

Directions 141

Slow Cooker Steak Fajitas 143

Ingredients 143

Directions 144

Best Whole Chicken in a Crockpot 145

Ingredients 145

Instructions 145

Thai Pork with Peanut Sauce 146

Ingredients 146

Possible garnishes 146

Directions 147

Slow Cooker Apple Cider Pork Roast 148

Ingredients 148

Directions 149

Slow Cooker Ham & White Beans 151

Instructions 151

Slow Cooker Cilantro Lime Chicken 152

Ingredients: 152

Directions 152

Pesto Lasagna with Spinach and Mushrooms 153

Ingredients 153

Preparation 153

Crock Pot Tuscan Chicken & Beans 155

Ingredients 155

Method 155

Crockpot Pineapple Chicken 156

Ingredients 156

Directions 156

Skinny Chicken Enchilads 158

Ingredients 158

Directions 159

Balsamic Roast Beef Recipe 160

Ingredients 160

Directions 160

Italian Stallion Crockpot Chicken 162

Ingredients 162

Dry Ingredients/Spices 162

Directions 163

Ginger Cranberry Pork Roast 164

Ingredients 164

Instructions 164

Pot Roast in the Crock Pot 166

Ingredients: 166

Directions: 167

Coconut Almond Cranberry Chicken 168

Ingredients 168

Directions 168

Crock Pot Orange Chicken 169

Ingredients 169

Instructions 169

Turkey Pad Thai Recipe 171

Ingredients 171

Directions 171

Turkey Lasagna 173

Ingredients 173

Directions 173

Clean Eating Crock Pot Chicken Tacos 175

Ingredients 175

Instructions 175

Italian Style Meatballs 177

Ingredients 177

Directions 177

Quinoa with Vegetables 179

Ingredients 179

Directions 180

Garlic Cauliflower Mashed Potatoes 181

Directions 181

Crock Pot Baked Potatoes 183

How To Make Crock Pot Baked Potatoes 183

Ingredients 183

Directions	183
Easy Chicken Stew	184
Ingredients	184
Directions	185
Tortellini Tuscan Stew	186
Ingredients	186
Directions	187
Sweet Potato and Apple Soup	188
Ingredients	188
Instructions	188
Slow-Cooker Chicken Tortilla Soup	190
Ingredients	190
Directions	190
Skinny Tomato Parmesan Tomato Basil Sout	192
Directions	193
Black Bean Soup with Chipotle and Toasted Cumin Seed Crème Fraîche	194
Ingredients	194
Directions	194
Toasted Cumin Seed Crème Fraîche	196
Ingredients	196

Directions 196

Slow Cooker Turkey Chili Recipe 197

Ingredients 197

How to do it 198

Slow Cooker Hearty Vegetable and Bean Soup 199

Ingredients 199

Directions 200

Tomato Basil Soup 201

Ingredients 201

Instructions 202

Hearty Chicken Stew with Butternut Squash & Quinoa Recipe 203

Ingredients 203

Instructions 203

Soy Ginger Soup 205

Ingredients 205

Directions 205

Farmer's market vegetable soup 206

Ingredients 206

Directions 207

Slow Cooker Savory Superfood Soup 208

Ingredients 208

Directions 209

Slow Cooker Savory Superfood Soup 210

Ingredients 210

Directions 210

Chicken Noodle Soup 211

Ingredients: 211

Directions 211

Vegetable and Chickpea Curry 212

Ingredients 212

Directions 212

Slow Cooker Fudge 213

Ingredients 213

Directions 213

Chicken Mole 215

Ingredients 215

Preparation 216

Honey Glazed Chicken Thighs 217

Ingredients 217

Preparation 217

Geoff's Easy Roast Chicken with Gravy

INGREDIENTS

- 1 chicken, roaster

- salt and pepper

PREPARATION

1.
We simply clean out the chicken, give it a wash then pop it in the crockpot. Add a pinch of salt and a sprinkle of pepper. Leave for about 6 hours on high.

2.
When we take the finished product out we drain the remaining juice into a mug, cover with foil and put it in the freezer for about half an hour. This solidifies all the fat at the top of the mug. Scrape this off and the stock that's left we add to the gravy.

Gingered Pineapple Chicken

INGREDIENTS

- 4 to 5 boneless chicken breast halves, cubed (about 3/4-inch)
- 1 bunch green onions, with about 3 inches of green sliced 1/2-inch
- 1 can (8oz) crushed pineapple, undrained
- 1 tablespoon finely chopped crystallized ginger
- 2 tablespoons lemon juice
- 2 tablespoons soy sauce (low sodium)
- 3 tablespoons brown sugar or honey
- 1/2 teaspoon garlic powder

PREPARATION

1. Combine all ingredients in the slow cooker; cover and cook on low for 6 to 8 hours. Serve over rice or flat noodles.

2. Serves 4.

Greek Chicken

INGREDIENTS

- 4 to 6 skinless chicken breasts

- 1 lg. can (15 ounces) tomato sauce

- 1 can (14.5 ounces) diced tomatoes with juice

- 1 can sliced mushrooms

- 1 can (4 ounces) sliced ripe olives

- 2 cloves garlic, minced

- 1 tbsp. lemon juice

- 1 tsp. dried leaf oregano

- 1/2 cup chopped onion

- 1/2 c. dry white wine (optional)

- 2 cups hot cooked rice

- Salt to taste

PREPARATION

1.
Wash chicken and pat dry. Bake in 350° oven for about 30 minutes. Meanwhile, combine all other ingredients (except rice). Dice chicken and combine with the sauce; cover and cook on low for 4 to 5 hours. Serve chicken and sauce with hot cooked rice.

2.
Serves 4 to 6.

Hawaiian Drumsticks

INGREDIENTS

- 12 chicken drumsticks

- 1 cup ketchup

- 1 cup packed dark brown sugar

- 1/2 cup soy sauce

- grated fresh ginger, 1 tablespoon

- a splash of sesame seed oil

PREPARATION

1.
Cover and crock on low for about 8 hours. Serve on top of white rice.

2.
Aloha!

3.
Chicken drumsticks recipe shared by LeRoy and the Nitz Dawg!

Herbed Chicken With Vegetables

INGREDIENTS

- 3 to 4 pounds chicken pieces
- 1 1/2 to 2 cups frozen or canned and drained small whole onions
- 2 cups whole baby carrots
- 2 medium potatoes, cut in 1-inch chunks
- 1 1/2 cups chicken broth
- 2 medium celery ribs, cut in 2-inch chunks
- 2 slices bacon, diced
- 1 bay leaf
- 1/4 teaspoon dried thyme
- 1/4 teaspoon black pepper
- 1/4 cup minced fresh parsley
- 2 tablespoons fresh tarragon, minced, or 1 teaspoon dried tarragon

- 1 teaspoon grated lemon peel

- 2 tablespoons fresh lemon juice

- 1/2 teaspoon salt, or to taste

PREPARATION

1.
In slow cooker, combine chicken, onions, carrots, potatoes, broth, celery, bacon, bay leaf, thyme and pepper. Set on low and cook 8 to 10 hours.

2.
Set aside.

3.
Remove chicken and vegetables to heated platter, using a slotted spoon. Cover with foil and keep warm. Skim off and discard excess fat. Stir in the parsley, tarragon, lemon zest and lemon juice, along with salt to taste; spoon over chicken and vegetables.

Herbed Chicken with Wild Rice

INGREDIENTS

- 1 to 1 1/2 pound chicken tenders or boneless chicken breast halves

- 6 to 8 ounces sliced mushrooms

- 1 tablespoon vegetable oil

- 2 to 3 slices crumbled bacon, or 2 tablespoons real bacon bits

- 1 teaspoon butter

- 1 (6 oz.) box Uncle Bens (chicken flavor) long grain and wild rice

- 1 can cream of of chicken soup, with herbs or plain

- 1 cup water

- 1 teaspoon herb mixture, such as fine herbes or a mixture of your favorites; parsley, thyme, tarragon, etc.

PREPARATION

1.
Saute chicken pieces and mushrooms in oil and butter until chicken is lightly browned. Place bacon on bottom of 3 1/2 to 5-quart slow cooker. Place rice over bacon. Reserve package of seasonings. Place chicken tenders over rice - if using chicken breasts, cut in strips or cubes. Pour soup over chicken, then add water. Top with seasonings and sprinkle with herb mixture. Cover and cook on LOW for 5 1/2 to 6 1/2 hours, or until rice is tender (not mushy).

2.
Serves 4 to 6.

Honey and Ginger Chicken

INGREDIENTS

- 3 pounds chicken breast halves without skin

- 1 1/4 inch fresh ginger root, peeled and finely chopped

- 2 cloves garlic, minced

- 1/2 cup soy sauce

- 1/2 cup honey

- 3 tablespoons dry sherry

- 2 tablespoons cornstarch blended with 2 tablespoons water

PREPARATION

1.

Combine ginger, garlic, soy sauce, honey, and sherry in a small bowl. Dip chicken pieces into sauce; place chicken pieces in slow cooker; pour remaining sauce over all. Cover and cook on LOW for about 6 hours.

2.

Remove chicken to warm serving dish and pour the liquids into a saute pan or skillet. Bring to a boil and continue simmering for 3 to 4 minutes to reduce slightly. Whisk the cornstarch into the sauce mixture.

3.

Cook over low heat until thickened. Pour a little sauce over chicken and pass remainder.

4.

Serve chicken with hot rice.

Honey Barbecued Chicken with Sweet Potatoes

INGREDIENTS

- 3 cups peeled and sliced sweet potatoes, about 2 medium to large sweet potatoes

- 1 can (8 ounces) pineapple chunks in juice, undrained

- 1/2 cup chicken broth

- 1/4 cup finely chopped onion

- 1/2 teaspoon ground ginger

- 1/3 cup barbecue sauce, your favorite

- 2 tablespoons honey

- 1/2 teaspoon dry mustard

- 4 to 6 chicken leg quarters (legs with thighs, skin removed

PREPARATION

1.

In 3 1/2 to 5-quart slow cooker, combine sweet potatoes, pineapple with juice, chicken broth, chopped onion, and ground ginger; stir to blend well. In small bowl, combine barbecue sauce, honey, and dry mustard; stir to blend well. Coat chicken generously on all sides barbecue sauce mixture. Arrange coated chicken in single layer over sweet potato and pineapple mixture, overlapping if necessary. Spoon any remaining barbecue sauce mixture over chicken.

2.

Cover; cook on low setting for 7 to 9 hours or until chicken is fork tender and juices run clear, and sweet potatoes are tender.

3.

Serves 4 to 6.

Honey Hoisin Chicken

INGREDIENTS

- 2 to 3 lbs chicken parts (or whole chicken, cut up)
- 2 tablespoons soy sauce
- 2 tablespoons hoisin sauce
- 2 tablespoons honey
- 2 tablespoons dry white wine
- 1 tablespoon grated ginger root or 1 teaspoon ground ginger
- 1/8 teaspoon ground black pepper
- 2 tablespoons cornstarch
- 2 tablespoons water

PREPARATION

1.
Wash chicken and pat dry; arrange in bottom of slow cooker.

2.
Combine soy sauce, hoisin sauce, honey, wine, ginger and pepper. Pour sauce over chicken.

3.
Cover and cook on low about 5 1/2 to 8 hours, or until chicken is tender and juices run clear.

4.
Mix cornstarch and water.

5.
Remove chicken from slow cooker; turn on high and add cornstarch and water mixture.

6.
Continue to cook until thickened, and add chicken back to slow cooker to heat through.

Italian Style Chicken

INGREDIENTS

- 4 chicken breasts, boneless, cut into bite size pieces

- 1 - 16 oz. can of tomatoes, chopped

- 1 large green sweet pepper, diced

- 1 small cooking onion, diced

- 1 medium rib of celery, diced

- 1 medium carrot, peeled and diced

- 1 bay leaf

- 1 teaspoon dried oregano

- 1 teaspoon dried basil

- 1/2 teaspoon dried thyme, optional

- 2 cloves of garlic, chopped; OR 2 tsp. garlic powder

- 1/2 teaspoon salt

- 1/2 teaspoon red pepper flakes, or to taste

- 1/2 cup grated Parmesan or Romano cheese

PREPARATION

1.
Combine all ingredients, except grated cheese, in slow cooker.

2.
Cover and cook on low for 6 to 8 hours. Remove bay leaf and sprinkle with grated cheese before serving.

3.
Good over rice or pasta.

Italian Style Chicken in the Crockpot

INGREDIENTS

- 1 pound boneless chicken thighs, skin removed, or 4 chicken leg quarters, skin removed

- 1/2 cup chopped onion

- 1/2 cup sliced pitted ripe olives

- 1 can (14.5-ounce) diced tomatoes, undrained

- 1 teaspoon dried leaf oregano

- 1/2 teaspoon salt

- 1/2 teaspoon dried rosemary, crumbled

- pinch dried leaf thyme

- 1/4 teaspoon garlic powder

- 1/4 cup cold water or chicken broth

- 1 tablespoon cornstarch

PREPARATION

1.

Place chicken in 3 1/2 to 5-quart slow cooker. Top with chopped onion and sliced olives. Combine tomatoes with oregano, salt, rosemary, thyme, and garlic powder. Pour tomato mixture over chicken. Cover and cook on LOW for 7 to 9 hours, or until chicken is fork tender and juices run clear. With slotted spoon, remove chicken and vegetables to a warm serving platter. Cover with foil and keep warm. Increase crockpot to HIGH.

2.

In cup or small bowl, combine water or broth and cornstarch; stir until smooth. Stir into liquids in the crockpot. Cover and cook until thickened. Serve thickened sauce with chicken.

3.

Serves 4.

Italian Style Chicken With Spaghetti, Slow Cooker

INGREDIENTS

- 1 can (8 ounces) tomato sauce
- 6 to 8 boneless chicken breast halves, skin removed
- 1 can (6 ounces) tomato paste
- 3 tablespoons water
- 3 medium cloves garlic, minced
- 2 teaspoons dried leaf oregano, crushed
- 1 teaspoon sugar, or to taste
- hot cooked spaghetti
- 4 ounces shredded mozzarella cheese
- grated Parmesan cheese

PREPARATION

1. If desired, brown the chicken in hot oil; drain. Sprinkle generously with salt and pepper. Arrange chicken in slow cooker. Combine tomato sauce, tomato paste, water, garlic, oregano and sugar; pour over the chicken. Cover and cook on LOW for 6 to 8 hours. Remove chicken and keep warm. Turn cooker to high heat setting, stir mozzarella cheese into sauce. Cook uncovered, till cheese melts and sauce is heated through.
2. Serve chicken and sauce over hot cooked spaghetti. Serve with Parmesan cheese.
3. Serves 6 to 8.

Light Chicken Stroganoff

INGREDIENTS

- 1 cup fat-free sour cream

- 1 tablespoon Gold Metal all-purpose flour

- 1 envelope chicken gravy mix (approximately 1 ounce)

- 1 cup water

- 1 pound boneless skinless chicken breast, cut into 1-inch pieces

- 16 ounces frozen California blend vegetables, thawed

- 1 cup sliced mushroom, sauteed

- 1 cup frozen peas

- 10 ounces potatoes, peeled and cut into 1-inch pieces, about 2 medium peeled potatoes

- 1 1/2 cups Bisquick baking mix

- 4 green onions, chopped (1/3 cups)

- 1/2 cup 1% low-fat milk

PREPARATION

1. Mix sour cream, flour, gravy mix and water in 3-1/2 to 5-quart crockpot until smooth. Stir in chicken, vegetables and mushrooms. Cover and cook on low heat setting 4 hours or until chicken in tender and sauce is thickened. Stir in peas. Mix baking mix and onions. Stir in milk just until moistened. Drop dough by rounded tablespoonfuls onto chicken-vegetables mixtures. Cover and cook on high heat setting 45 to 50 minutes or until toothpick inserted in center of dumplings coming out clean.
2. Serve immediately 4 Servings.

Lilly's Slow Cooker Chicken With Cheese Sauce

INGREDIENTS

- 6 boneless, skinless chicken breast halves

- 2 cans cream of chicken soup

- 1 can cheese soup

- salt, pepper, garlic powder to taste

PREPARATION

1. Sprinkle chicken breasts with garlic powder, salt, and pepper.
2. Place 3 chicken breasts in slow cooker. Combine all soups; pour half of the soup over the first 3 chicken breasts.
3. Place the remaining 3 chicken breasts on top. Pour remaining soup over the top.
4. Cover and cook on LOW for 6 to 8 hours.

Mexican-Style Chicken Breasts

INGREDIENTS

- 2 tablespoons vegetable oil
- 3 to 4 boneless chicken breast halves, without skin, cut into 1-inch pieces
- 1/2 cup chopped onion
- 1 green bell pepper (or use a red bell pepper)
- 1 to 2 small jalapeno peppers, finely chopped
- 3 cloves garlic, minced
- 1 can (4 ounces) mild chile peppers, chopped
- 1 can (14 1/2 ounce) Mexican style, chili style, or fire-roasted diced tomatoes
- 1 teaspoon dried leaf oregano
- 1/4 teaspoon ground cumin
- shredded Mexican blend cheese
- salsa

Optional Garnishes

- sour cream

- guacamole

- sliced green onions

- diced tomatoes

- shredded lettuce

- sliced ripe olives

- cilantro

PREPARATION

1. Heat oil in a large skillet over medium heat. Brown chicken breasts. Remove and drain.
2. In the same skillet, sauté onion, green bell pepper, garlic and jalapeno pepper just until tender.
3. Put the chicken breasts and onion mixture in the slow cooker.
4. Add mild chile peppers, tomatoes, oregano, and cumin to the slow cooker; stir to combine.

5. Cover and cook on LOW 6 to 8 hours (HIGH 3 to 4 hours).
6. Serve with warm flour tortillas, shredded cheese, and salsa, along with your favorite toppings and condiments.
7. Guacamole or sour cream would make a nice garnish with sliced green onions or diced tomatoes.

Paula's Chicken With Leeks

INGREDIENTS

- 3 to 4 pounds chicken parts, bone-in
- 4 to 6 potatoes, sliced about 1/4-inch thick
- 1 package leek soup mix
- 1 thinly sliced leek or 4 sliced green onions
- 1/2 to 1 cup water
- paprika
- Seasonings

PREPARATION

1. Layer potatoes in bottom of slow cooker/Crock Pot, top with onion or leek, and then add chicken. (If you will have several layers of chicken, salt and pepper bottom layers as you put them in. Don't season top layer yet.) Mix leek soup with approximately 1/2 cup water; pour over all. Season top layer of chicken. At this point, I also sprinkle with paprika to give it color.

• If you like, add minced garlic and some fresh rosemary to season.

Cook on low for 6 to 7 hours, adding more water if needed.

Saucy Jack Daniel's Barbecue Chicken Drumettes

INGREDIENTS

- 5 to 6 pounds chicken drumettes

- 1 cup all-purpose flour

- 1 teaspoon salt

- 1/2 teaspoon ground black pepper

-

Barbecue Sauce

- 1 1/2 cups ketchup

- 4 tablespoons butter

- 1/2 cup Jack Daniels or other good quality whisky

- 5 tablespoons brown sugar

- 3 tablespoons molasses

- 3 tablespoons cider vinegar

- 2 tablespoons Worcestershire sauce

- 1 tablespoon soy sauce

- 4 teaspoons Dijon style mustard or a gourmet mustard

- 2 teaspoons liquid smoke

- 1 1/2 teaspoons onion powder

- 1 teaspoon garlic powder

- 1 tablespoon sriracha, or more, to taste (may substitute about 1 scant teaspoon cayenne pepper)

- 1/2 teaspoon ground black pepper

PREPARATION

1. Line 2 rimmed baking sheets with foil; spray with nonstick cooking spray. Heat the oven to 425°.
2. Toss the drumettes with a mixture of the flour, 1 teaspoon of salt, and 1/2 teaspoon of pepper.
3. Arrange on the baking sheets and bake for 20 minutes. Turn the drumettes and return to the oven. Bake for 20 minutes longer, or until nicely browned.
4. Meanwhile, put all sauce ingredients in a medium saucepan; mix well and bring to a boil over medium heat.
5. Reduce heat and simmer for 5 minutes.
6. Transfer the drumettes to a bowl or slow cooker insert (if you'll be keeping them warm for a party). Toss with about half of the barbecue sauce. Serve immediately with the sauce or turn the slow cooker on LOW to keep them warm. If not serving immediately, refrigerate the remaining sauce until serving time.
7. Serve the drumettes hot with the sauce for dipping. Have plenty of napkins on hand.
8. This recipe makes about 3 dozen pieces, enough for 6 to 8 people as an appetizer..

Sherri's Chicken & Dumplings

INGREDIENTS

- 4 chicken breast halves

- 2 cans chicken broth (3 1/2 cups)

- 1 cup water

- 3 cubes chicken bouillon or equivalent base or granules

- 1 small carrot, chopped

- 1 small rib celery, chopped

- 1/2 cup chopped onion

- 12 large flour tortillas

PREPARATION

1. Combine all ingredients in slow cooker, except tortillas. Cook on low 8 to 10 hours. Take out chicken and remove meat from bones, then place broth on stove in large pot. Cut chicken into bite-size pieces and return to broth on stovetop. Bring to a slow boil.
2. Cut tortillas in half, then in 1-inch strips. Place strips into simmering broth and boil gently for 15 to 20 minutes, stir occasionally. Broth should thicken but if too thin, combine 1 tablespoon cornstarch with just enough water to dissolve and stir into broth.
3. Cook 5 to 10 minutes more.
4. Serves 4.

Simple Slow Cooker Chicken Barbecue

INGREDIENTS

- 3 boneless chicken breast halves

- 1 1/2 cups spicy barbecue sauce, your choice, plus more for serving

- 1 medium onion, sliced or chopped

- toasted buns

- coleslaw, for serving

PREPARATION

1. Wash the chicken breasts and pat dry. Put in a slow cooker with 1 1/2 cups of barbecue sauce and the onion. Stir to coat the chicken. Cover and cook on HIGH for 3 hours.
2. Remove the chicken breasts to a plate and shred or chop. Return the shredded chicken to the sauce in the slow cooker; stir to blend. Cover and cook for 10 minutes longer.
3. Serve the shredded chicken on toasted buns with coleslaw and extra barbecue sauce.
4. Serves 4 to 6.

Slow-Cooked Chicken Dijon

INGREDIENTS

- 1 to 2 pounds chicken breast tenders

- 1 can condensed cream of chicken soup, undiluted (10 1/2 ounce)

- 2 tablespoons regular or grainy Dijon mustard

- 1 tablespoon cornstarch

- 1/2 cup water

- pepper to taste

- 1 teaspoon dried parsley flakes or 1 tablespoon fresh chopped parsley

PREPARATION

1. Wash chicken and pat dry; arrange in the slow cooker. Combine the soup with mustard and cornstar; add water and stir. Stir in parsley and pepper. Pour the mixture over the chicken. Cover and cook on LOW for 6 to 7 hours. Serve with hot cooked rice and a side vegetable.
2. Chicken Dijon recipe serves 4 to 6.

Slow Cooker Barbecue Chicken

INGREDIENTS

- 3 to 4 pounds chicken pieces

- 1 large onion, coarsely chopped

- 1 bottle barbecue sauce

PREPARATION

1. Put chicken in bottom of slow cooker or crockpot and add onions and barbecue sauce. Cook on LOW for about 6 to 8 hours, or until chicken is tender but not falling apart.
2. Serves 4 to 6.

Slow Cooker Barbecued Chicken Thighs

INGREDIENTS

- 1/2 cup flour
- 1/2 teaspoon garlic powder
- 1 teaspoon dry mustard
- 1 teaspoon salt
- 1/4 teaspoon pepper
- 8 chicken thighs
- 2 tablespoons vegetable oil
- 1 cup thick barbecue sauce

PREPARATION

1. Put flour, garlic powder, mustard, salt, and pepper in a food storage bag. Add chicken, a few pieces at a time, and shake to coat thoroughly. Heat oil in large skillet; add chicken and brown on all sides. Put half of the barbecue sauce in crockpot; add chicken then add remaining sauce. Cook on low 6 to 7 hours, or until chicken is tender and juices run clear.
2. Serves 4 to 6.

Slow Cooker Chicken and Sausage Pasta Sauce

INGREDIENTS

- 1 tablespoon olive oil
- 4 garlic cloves, crushed
- 1/2 cup chopped onion
- 1 red bell pepper, chopped
- 1 green bell pepper, chopped
- 1 small zucchini, chopped
- 1 can (4 ounces) mushrooms
- 1 can stewed tomatoes, Italian seasoned
- 1 can (6 ounces) tomato paste
- 3 sweet Italian sausage links
- 4 boneless chicken breast halves, cut in strips
- 1 teaspoon Italian seasoning

- red pepper flakes, to taste, optional

PREPARATION

1. Heat oil in skillet. Saute onion and garlic until light brown. Remove.
2. Add sausage; brown on all sides. Add chicken and cook just until browned. Drain off excess fat. Slice sausages in 1-inch pieces. In slow cooker combine all remaining ingredients with the onions and garlic. Add the sausage then top with the chicken strips. Cover and cook on LOW 4 to 6 hours, until chicken is tender but not dry.
3. Serve this tasty sauce over hot cooked pasta.
4. Serves 4.

Slow Cooker Chicken Curry

INGREDIENTS

- 2 whole chicken breasts, boned and diced
- 1 can cream of chicken soup
- 1/4 cup dry sherry
- 2 tbsp. butter or margarine
- 2 green onions with tops, finely chopped
- 1/4 tsp. curry powder
- 1 tsp. salt
- Dash of pepper
- hot cooked rice

PREPARATION

1. Place chicken in crockpot. Add all remaining ingredients, except rice. Cover and cook on Low for 4 to 6 hours, or on HIGH 2 to 3 hours. Serve over hot rice.

Slow Cooker Chicken Curry With Rice

INGREDIENTS

- 4 boneless, skinless chicken breasts, cut in 1 inch strips or chunks
- 2 large onions, quartered and sliced thinly
- 3 cloves garlic, minced
- 1 tablespoon soy sauce or Tamari
- 1 teaspoon Madras curry powder
- 2 teaspoons chili powder
- 1 teaspoon turmeric
- 1 teaspoon ground ginger
- 1/3 cup chicken broth or water
- salt and freshly ground black pepper, to taste
- hot cooked rice

PREPARATION

1. Mix all ingredients, except rice, together in the slow cooker or /Crock Pot.
2. Cover and cook on low from 6 to 8 hours, or until chicken is tender.
3. Taste and season with salt and pepper, as needed.
4. Serve over rice or noodles

Slow Cooker Chicken Enchiladas

INGREDIENTS

- 3 cups diced cooked chicken

- 3 cups shredded Mexican blend cheese with peppers, divided

- 1 can (4.5 ounces) chopped green chile peppers

- 1/4 cup chopped fresh cilantro

- 1 1/2 cups sour cream, divided

- 8 flour tortillas (8 inch)

- 1 cup tomatillo salsa

- Suggested Garnishes: diced tomatoes, sliced green onions, ripe olives, jalapeno rings, chopped fresh cilantro

PREPARATION

1. Lightly grease the crockery insert of a 4- to 6-quart slow cooker.
2. In a bowl combine the diced chicken with 2 cups of the shredded cheese, chopped green chile peppers, 1/4 cup chopped cilantro, and 1/2 cup of sour cream; stir to blend ingredients.
3. Spoon some chicken mixture down the center of the tortillas, dividing mixture evenly among all eight tortillas. Roll them up and arrange, seam side down, in the prepared slow cooker.
4. If necessary, stack the tortillas.
5. In a small bowl, combine the salsa with the remaining 1 cup of sour cream. Spoon the mixture over the tortillas.
6. Cover and cook on LOW for 4 hours. Sprinkle the tortillas with the remaining shredded cheese. Cover and cook on LOW for about 20 to 30 minutes longer.
7. Serves 4 to 6.

Slow Cooker Chicken Fricassee With Vegetables

INGREDIENTS

- 4 to 6 boneless chicken breast halves, skin removed
- salt and pepper to taste
- 2 tablespoons butter
- 2 cloves garlic, minced
- 3 tablespoons all-purpose flour
- 2 cups low sodium chicken broth
- 1 teaspoon dried leaf thyme
- 1/2 teaspoon dried leaf tarragon
- 3 to 4 carrots, cut in 2-inch pieces
- 2 onions, halved, thickly sliced
- 2 large leeks, white part only, washed and chopped
- 1 bay leaf

- 1/2 cup half-and-half or light cream

- 1 1/2 cups frozen peas, thawed

PREPARATION

1. Wash chicken breasts and pat dry. Set aside. Saute minced garlic in butter for a minute, then add flour and cook, stirring, until smooth. Pour in broth (you can use 1/4 cup of dry white wine or sherry in place of some of the broth), the thyme and tarragon, and stir until thickened. Layer in the Crock Pot the onions, carrots, chicken, then leeks; pour sauce over all. Add bay leaf. Cover and cook on LOW for 6 to 7 hours, or on HIGH for 3 to 5 hours.
2. If cooking on low, change to high and stir in half and half and thawed peas. Cover and continue cooking on high another 15 minutes, or until peas are heated through. Taste and adjust seasonings. Remove bay leaf before serving.
3. Serves 4 to 6.

Slow Cooker Chicken in Spicy Sauce

INGREDIENTS

- 1/2 c. tomato juice

- 1/2 c. soy sauce

- 1/2 c. brown sugar

- 1/4 c. chicken broth

- 3 garlic cloves, minced

- 3 to 4 pounds chicken pieces, skin removed

PREPARATION

1. Combine all ingredients except chicken in a deep bowl. Dip each piece of chicken in the sauce. Place in the slow cooker. Pour remaining sauce over the top. Cook on low for 6 to 8 hours or high for 3 to 4 hours.
2. Makes 6 servings.

Slow Cooker Chicken Madras With Curry Powder

INGREDIENTS

- 3 onions, thinly sliced

- 4 apples, peeled, cored and thinly sliced

- 1 teaspoon salt

- 1 to 2 teaspoons curry powder, or to taste

- 1 frying chicken, cut up

- paprika

PREPARATION

1. In crockpot, combine onion and apples; sprinkle with salt and curry powder. Mix well. Arrange chicken skin down over onion mixture. sprinkle generously with paprika.
2. Cover and cook on LOW for 6 to 8 hours, until chicken is tender.
3. Taste and add more seasonings, if needed.
4. Serves 4.

Slow Cooker Chicken With Mushrooms

INGREDIENTS

- 6 bone-in chicken breast halves, skin removed
- 1 1/4 teaspoons salt
- 1/4 teaspoon pepper
- 1/4 teaspoon paprika
- 1 3/4 teaspoons chicken flavored bouillon granules or chicken base
- 1 1/2 cups sliced fresh mushrooms
- 1/2 cup green onions, sliced, with green
- 1/2 cup dry white wine
- 1/2 cup evaporated milk
- 5 teaspoons cornstarch
- fresh chopped parsley

PREPARATION

1. Wash chicken and pat dry. In a bowl, combine salt, pepper and paprika. Rub over all sides of chicken, using all of the mixture. In a slow cooker, alternate layers of chicken, bouillon granules or base, mushrooms and green onions. Pour wine slowly over top. Do not stir ingredients. Cover and cook on high for 2 1/2 to 3 hours or on low for 5 to 6 hours or until chicken is tender but not falling apart.
2. With a slotted spoon, remove chicken and vegetables to a serving platter or bowl. Cover with foil and keep chicken warm. In a small saucepan, combine evaporated milk and cornstarch, stirring until smooth. Gradually stir in 2 cups of the cooking liquid. Stirring over medium heat, bring to a boil; continue to boi for 1 minute, or until thickened. Spoon some of the sauce over chicken and garnish with parsley, if desired. Serve with hot cooked rice or noodles, if desired.

Slow Cooker Cordon Bleu

INGREDIENTS

- 6 chicken breast halves, boneless, skinless - pounded to flatten slightly
- 6 thin slices ham
- 6 thin slices Swiss cheese
- 1/4 to 1/2 cup flour, for coating
- 1/2 pound sliced mushrooms
- 1/2 cup chicken broth
- 1/2 cup dry white wine (or use chicken broth)
- 1/2 teaspoon rosemary, crushed
- 1/4 cup grated Parmesan cheese
- 2 teaspoons cornstarch mixed with 1 tablespoon cool water
- salt and pepper to taste

PREPARATION

1. Place a slice of ham and slice of cheese on each flattened chicken breast and roll up. Secure with toothpicks and roll each in flour to coat. Place mushrooms in the slow cooker, then the chicken breasts. Whisk together the broth, wine (if using), and rosemary; pour over chicken. Sprinkle with the Parmesan cheese. Cover and cook on low for 6 to 7 hours. Just before serving, remove the chicken; keep warm.
2. To juices in slow cooker, add cornstarch mixture; stir until thickened. Salt and pepper, then taste and adjust seasonings. Pour sauce over chicken rolls and serve.
3. Serves 6.

Slow Cooker Dijon Chicken

INGREDIENTS

- 4 boneless chicken breast halves

- 1 heaping tablespoon honey Dijon mustard

- salt and coarsely ground black pepper or seasoned pepper

- 2 packages (8 ounces each) baby spinach, or 1 pound washed and dried fresh spinach leaves

- 2 tablespoons butter, cut in small pieces

- chopped fresh cilantro or parsley, optional

- toasted sliced almonds, optional•

PREPARATION

1. Grease the crockery insert of the slow cooker or spray with nonstick cooking spray.
2. Wash chicken breasts and pat dry.
3. Rub the chicken with the honey mustard; sprinkle with salt and pepper.
4. Arrange the chicken breasts in the crockery insert of the slow cooker. Top with spinach.
5. If your slow cooker is too small for all of the spinach, steam it briefly and add the wilted spinach leaves.

6. Dot spinach with butter and sprinkle with more salt and pepper.
7.
8. Garnish with cilantro or parsley or sprinkle with toasted almonds before serving, if desired.
9. Cover and cook on LOW for 5 to 6 hours.

•To toast almonds, add to a dry skillet over medium heat. Cook, constantly stirring, until lightly browned and aromatic.

Slow Cooker Lemon Chicken

INGREDIENTS

- 1 broiler-fryer, cut up, or about 3 1/2 pounds chicken pieces

- 1 teaspoon crumbled dry leaf oregano

- 2 cloves garlic, minced

- 2 tablespoons butter

- 1/4 cup dry wine, sherry, chicken broth, or water

- 3 tablespoons lemon juice

- Salt and pepper

PREPARATION

1. Season the chicken pieces with salt and pepper. Sprinkle half of garlic and oregano over the chicken.
2. Melt butter in a sauté pan over medium heat and brown chicken on all sides.
3. Transfer chicken to crockpot. Sprinkle with remaining oregano and garlic. Add wine or sherry to the sauté pan and stir to loosen brown bits; pour into slow cooker.
4. Cover and cook on LOW (200°) for 7 to 8 hours. Add lemon juice last hour.
5. Skim fat from juices and pour to a serving bowl; thicken juices, if desired.
6. Serve chicken with juices.
7. Serves 4.

Slow Cooker Pulled Chicken

INGREDIENTS

- 1 tablespoon butter

- 1 cup chopped onions

- 1/2 teaspoon minced garlic

- 1 1/2 cups tomato ketchup

- 1/2 cup apricot preserves, or peach preserves

- 3 tablespoons cider vinegar

- 2 tablespoons Worcestershire sauce

- 2 teaspoons liquid smoke

- 2 tablespoons molasses

- dash allspice

- 1/4 teaspoon freshly ground black pepper

- 1/8 to 1/4 teaspoon ground cayenne pepper

- 1 pound boneless chicken breasts

- 1 pound boneless chicken thighs

PREPARATION

1. In a medium saucepan over medium heat, melt the butter. When the butter is foamy, add the chopped onions and cook, stirring, until the onions are softened and lightly browned. Add the minced garlic and cook, stirring, for about 1 minute longer. Add the ketchup, apricot preserves, vinegar, Worcestershire sauce, liquid smoke, molasses, allspice, black pepper, and cayenne. Simmer for 5 minutes.
2. Put 1 1/2 cups of the sauce in the crockery insert of the slow cooker.
3. Reserve the remaining sauce; put in a container and refrigerate until serving time. Add the chicken pieces to the slow cooker. Cover and cook on LOW for 4 1/2 to 5 hours, or until the chicken is very tender and shreds easily. Using a fork, shred the chicken pieces.
4. Serve on split toasted buns with coleslaw and the extra extra barbecue sauce.
5. A menu might also include potato salad or baked potatoes, along with baked beans and sliced pickles and tomatoes. I like coleslaw and pickles on my barbecue, but other toppings might include jalapeno pepper rings, thinly sliced red onion, plain shredded cabbage, and sliced tomatoes or cucumbers.
6. Serves 8.

Smoked Sausage and Cabbage

INGREDIENTS

- 1 small head cabbage, coarsely shredded

- 1 large onion, coarsely chopped

- 1 1/2 to 2 pounds turkey Polish or smoked sausage kielbasa, cut in 1 to 2-inch pieces

- 1 cup apple juice

- 1 tablespoon dijon mustard

- 1 tablespoon cider vinegar

- 1 to 2 tablespoons brown sugar

- 1 teaspoon caraway seed, optional

- pepper, to taste

PREPARATION

1. Layer the cabbage, onion, and sausage in a 5- or 6-quart slow cooker (to make in a 3 1/2-quart cooker, use less cabbage or wilt it by boiling about 10 minutes, then drain and add). Whisk together the juice, mustard, vinegar, brown sugar, and caraway seed, if used; pour over slow cooker ingredients. Sprinkle with pepper, to taste. Cover and cook on low for 8 to 10 hours. Serve with potatoes and a tossed green salad, if desired.

Spanish Chicken With Rice

INGREDIENTS

- 4 chicken breast halves, skin removed
- 1/4 teaspoon salt
- 1/4 teaspoon pepper
- 1/4 teaspoon paprika
- 1 tablespoon vegetable oil
- 1 medium onion, chopped
- 1 small red pepper, chopped (or chopped roasted red pepper)
- 3 cloves garlic, minced
- 1/2 teaspoon dried rosemary
- 1 can (14 1/2 oz) crushed tomatoes
- 1 package (10 oz) frozen peas

PREPARATION

1. Season chicken with salt, pepper, paprika. In skillet, heat oil over medium heat and brown chicken on all sides. Transfer the chicken to slow cooker.
2. In a small bowl combine remaining ingredients, except frozen peas. Pour over chicken. Cover and cook on low 7 to 9 hours or on high 3 to 4 hours. One hour before serving, rinse peas in colander under warm water to thaw then add to crockpot. Serve this chicken dish over hot cooked rice.

Tami's Barbecued Chicken Legs

INGREDIENTS

- 6 to 8 frozen chicken legs
- 1 bottle thick barbecue sauce

PREPARATION

1. Put frozen chicken legs in slow cooker. Pour BBQ sauce over them. Cover and cook on HIGH for 6 to 8 hours.
2. •Note: If starting with thawed chicken legs, you may remove skin or brown first to reduce fat, and cook on LOW for 6 to 8 hours.

Tami's Crockpot Chicken Mozzarella

INGREDIENTS

- 4 chicken leg quarters

- 2 tablespoons garlic pepper seasoning

- 1 can zucchini with tomato sauce

- 4 ounces shredded Mozzarella cheese

PREPARATION

1. Arrange the chicken in the slow cooker and sprinkle with seasoning. Pour zucchini with tomato sauce over chicken. Cover and cook on LOW for 6 to 8 hours. Sprinkle with cheese and cook until cheese melts, about 30 minutes.

White Chicken Chili

INGREDIENTS

- 4 boneless chicken breast halves, skin removed, cut in 1/2-inch pieces
- 1/2 cup chopped celery
- 1/2 cup chopped onion
- 2 cans (14.5 ounces each) stewed tomatoes, cut up
- 16 oz. med. salsa or picante sauce
- 1 can chick peas or Great Northern beans, drained
- 6 to 8 oz. sliced mushrooms
- Olive oil

PREPARATION

1. Brown chicken in 1 tablespoon olive oil. Chop celery, onion and mushrooms. Combine all ingredients in large slow cooker; stir and simmer on low heat for 6 to 8 hours. Serve with crusty bread or taco chips. •If you like it spicy, use hot salsa or picante sauce.

Slow Cooker Chicken and Black Beans

INGREDIENTS

- 3 to 4 boneless chicken breast halves, cut in strips

- 1 can (12 to 15 ounces) corn, drained

- 1 can (15 oz) black beans, rinsed and drained

- 2 teaspoons gound cumin

- 2 teaspoons chili powder

- 1 onion, halved and thinly sliced

- 1 green bell pepper, cut in strips

- 1 can (14.5 ounces) diced tomatoes

- 1 can (6 ounces) tomato paste

PREPARATION

1. Combine all ingredients in slow cooker. Cover and cook on low for 5 to 6 hours.
2. Garnish with shredded cheese, if desired. Serve fiesta chicken and black beans with warmed flour tortillas, or over rice.
3. Serves 4.

Chicken and Dressing, Slow Cooker

INGREDIENTS

- 1 bag seasoned stuffing mix, 14 to 16 ounces
- 3 to 4 cups cooked diced chicken
- 3 cans cream of chicken soup
- 1/2 cup milk
- 1 to 2 cups mild cheddar cheese, shredded

PREPARATION

1. Prepare stuffing mix according to package directions and place in 5 quart Crock Pot. Stir in 2 cans of Cream of Chicken soup. In a mixing bowl, stir together cubed chicken, 1 can cream of chicken soup and milk. Spread over stuffing in slow cooker. Sprinkle cheese over top. Cover and cook on Low for 4 to 6 hour or on High for 2 to 3 hours.
2. Serves 6 to 8.

Chicken and Mushrooms, Slow Cooker

INGREDIENTS

- 6 chicken breast halves, bone-in, skin removed
- 1 1/4 tsp. salt
- 1/4 tsp. pepper
- 1/4 tsp. paprika
- 2 teaspoons chicken bouillon granules
- 1 1/2 cup sliced mushrooms
- 1/2 cup sliced green onions
- 1/2 cup dry white wine
- 2/3 cup evaporated milk
- 5 tsp. cornstarch
- Minced fresh parsley
- hot cooked rice

PREPARATION

1. In a small bowl, mix salt, pepper and paprika. Rub all of the mixture into the chicken.
2. In a slow cooker, alternate layers of chicken, bouillon granules, mushrooms, and green onions. Pour wine over top. DO NOT STIR.
3. Cover and cook on HIGH for 2 1/2 to 3 hours or on LOW for 5 to 6 hours, or until chicken is tender but not falling off bone. Baste one about halfway through cooking if possible.
4. Remove chicken and vegetables to a platter with a slotted spoon.
5. Cover with foil and keep warm.
6. In a small saucepan, combine evaporated milk and cornstarch until smooth. Gradually stir in 2 cups of the cooking liquid. Stirring over medium heat, bring to a boil and boil for 1 to 2 minutes, or until thickened.
7. Spoon some of the sauce over chicken and garnish with minced parsley. Serve remaining sauce on the side.
8. Serve with hot cooked rice.

Chicken and Rice Parmesan, Slow Cooker

INGREDIENTS

- 1 envelope onion soup mix

- 1 can (10 3/4 ounces) condensed cream of mushroom soup, reduced fat

- 1 can (10 3/4 ounces) condensed cream of chicken soup, reduced fat

- 1 1/2 cups low or no fat milk

- 1 cup dry white wine

- 1 cup white rice

- 6 boneless chicken breast halves, without skin

- 2 tablespoons butter

- 2/3 cup grated Parmesan cheese

PREPARATION

1. Mix onion soup, condensed cream soups, milk, wine and rice. Spray Crock Pot w/pam. Lay chicken breasts in Crock Pot, top with 1 teaspoon of butter, pour soup mixture over all, then sprinkle with the Parmesan cheese. Cook on low 8 to 10 hours or on high for 4 to 6 hours. Serves 6.

Chicken and Shrimp

INGREDIENTS

- 2 pounds chicken, boneless thighs and breasts, skin removed, cut in chunks
- 2 tablespoons of extra virgin olive oil
- 1 cup chopped onion
- 2 cloves garlic, minced
- 1/4 cup parsley, minced
- 1/2 cup white wine
- 1 large can (15 ounces) tomato sauce
- 1 teaspoon dried leaf basil
- 1 pound uncooked shrimp, peeled and deveined
- salt and freshly ground black pepper, to taste
- 1 pound fettuccine, linguine, or spaghetti

PREPARATION

1. In a large skillet or sauté pan over medium heat, heat the olive oil. Add the chicken chunks and cook, stirring, until lightly browned. Remove chicken to slow cooker.
2. Add a little more oil to the pan and sauté the onion, garlic, and parsley for about 1 minute. Remove from heat and stir in the wine, tomato sauce, and dried basil. Pour the mixture over chicken in slow cooker.
3. Cover and cook on LOW for 4 to 5 hours.
4. Stir in shrimp, cover, and cook on LOW for about 1 hour longer.
5. Season with salt and freshly ground black pepper, to taste.
6. Just before the dish is done, cook the pasta in boiling salted water as directed on the package.

Chicken and Stuffing Recipe

INGREDIENTS

- 4 boneless chicken breast halves, without skin
- 4 slices Swiss cheese
- 1 can (10 1/2 ounce) condensed cream of chicken soup
- 1 can (10 1/2 ounce) condensed cream of mushroom soup
- 1 cup chicken broth
- 1/4 cup milk
- 2 to 3 cups Pepperidge Farm Herb Stuffing Mix or Homemade Stuffing Mix
- 1/2 cup melted butter •See Sandy's Notes
- salt and pepper to taste

PREPARATION

1. Season chicken breasts with salt and pepper; place chicken breasts slow cooker.

2. Pour chicken broth over chicken breasts.

3.
Put one slice of Swiss cheese on each breast.

4.
Combine both cans of soup and milk. Cover chicken breasts with soup mixture.

5.
Sprinkle stuffing mix over all. Drizzle melted butter on top.

6.
Cook on low for 6-8 hours.

Chicken Breasts in Creamy Creole Sauce

INGREDIENTS

- 1 bunch green onions (6 to 8, with most of the green part)
- 2 slices bacon
- 1 teaspoon Creole or Cajun seasoning
- 3 tablespoons butter
- 4 tablespoons flour
- 3/4 cup chicken broth
- 1 to 2 tablespoons tomato paste
- 4 boneless chicken breast halves
- 1/4 to 1/2 cup half and half or milk

PREPARATION

1. In a saucepan, melt butter over medium low heat. Add onions and bacon, cook and stir for 2 minutes. Add flour, stir and cook for 2 more minutes. Add chicken broth; cook until thick then add tomato paste. Place chicken breasts in the slow cooker/Crock Pot; add sauce mixture. Cover and cook on low for 6 to 7 hours, stirring after 3 hours. Stir in milk about 20 to 30 minutes before done. Serve over pasta or rice.
2. Serves 4.

Chicken Chili with Hominy

INGREDIENTS

- 2 pounds chicken breasts, boneless and skinless, cut in 1 to 1 1/2-inch pieces
- 1 medium onion, chopped
- 3 cloves garlic, thinly sliced
- 1 can (15 oz) white hominy, drained
- 1 can (14 oz) diced tomatoes, undrained
- 1 can (28 oz) tomatillos, drained and chopped
- 1 can (4 oz) mild green chiles

PREPARATION

1. Combine all ingredients in slow cooker; stir to blend all ingredients. Cover and cook on low for 7 to 9 hours, or high for 4 to 4 1/2 hours.
2. Serves 4 to 6.

Chicken Delish

INGREDIENTS

- 6 to 8 boneless, skinless chicken breast halves
- lemon juice
- salt and pepper, to taste
- celery salt or seasoned salt, to taste
- paprika, to taste
- 1 can cream of celery soup
- 1 can cream of mushroom soup
- 1/3 cup dry white wine
- grated Parmesan cheese, to taste
- cooked rice

PREPARATION

1. Rinse chicken; pat dry. Season with lemon juice, salt, pepper, celery salt, and paprika. Place chicken in slow cooker. In medium bowl mix soups with wine. Pour over chicken breasts. Sprinkle with Parmesan cheese. Cover and cook on low for 6 to 8 hours. Serve chicken with sauce over hot cooked rice, and pass the Parmesan cheese.
2. Serves 4 to 6.

Chicken Enchiladas for the Slow Cooker

INGREDIENTS

- 1 pkg. chicken breasts (1 - 1 1/2 lbs)

- 1 jar chicken gravy

- 1 4 oz can green chiles, chopped

- 1 onion, chopped

- corn tortillas

- shredded cheese

PREPARATION

1. Combine chicken, gravy, green chiles, and chopped onion in slow cooker; cover and cook on LOW for 5 to 6 hours. Take chicken out of sauce and shred. Fill corn tortillas with chicken and sauce. Top with shredded cheese and roll. Place in baking dish. Pour excess sauce over and sprinkle with more shredded cheese. Bake at 350° for approximately 15 to 20 minutes.
2. Serves 4 to 6.

Chicken Las Vegas

INGREDIENTS

- 6 boneless chicken breast halves, without skin

- 1 can cream of mushroom soup

- 1/2 pint. sour cream

- 1 (6 oz.) jar dried, chipped beef

PREPARATION

1. Mix together soup, sour cream and dried beef. Roll chicken in the mixture, coating well; place in crockpot. Pour remaining mixture over chicken. Cover and cook on LOW for 5 to 7 hours, until chicken is tender but not dried out. Serve with hot cooked rice or noodles.
2. Serves 6.

Chicken Parisienne for the Slow Cooker

INGREDIENTS

- 6 to 8 chicken breast halves
- salt, pepper, and paprika
- 1/2 cup dry white wine
- 1 (10 1/2 oz.) can cream of mushroom soup
- 8 ounces sliced mushrooms
- 1 cup sour cream
- 1/4 cup flour

PREPARATION

1. Sprinkle chicken breasts with salt, pepper and paprika. Place in slow cooker. Mix wine, soup and mushrooms until well combined. Pour over chicken. Sprinkle with paprika. Cover and cook on low for 6 to 8 hours, or until chicken is tender but not too dry. Mix sour cream and flour together; add to the Crock Pot. Cook for about 20 minutes longer, until heated through.
2. Serve with rice or noodles.
3. Serves 6 to 8.

Chicken Reuben Casserole, Slow Cooker

INGREDIENTS

- 32 ounces sauerkraut (jar or bag), rinsed and drained
- 1 cup Russian dressing
- 4 to 6 boneless chicken breast halves, skin removed
- 1 tablespoon prepared mustard
- 1 cup shredded Swiss cheese or Monterey Jack

PREPARATION

1. Layer half of the sauerkraut in the bottom of the pot. Pour 1/3 cup dressing over it; place 2 to 3 chicken breasts on top and spread the mustard on chicken. Top with the remaining sauerkraut and chicken breasts; pour another 1/3 cup of dressing over all and reserve the remaining 1/3 cup of dressing for serving.
2. Cover and cook on low for about 4 hours, or until chicken is cooked through and tender. Sprinkle Swiss cheese and cook until cheese is melted.
3. Serve with reserved dressing.
4. Serves 4 to 6.

Chicken with Cranberries

INGREDIENTS

- 6 boneless, skinless chicken breasts
- 1 small onion, chopped
- 1 cup fresh cranberries
- 1 teaspoon salt
- 1/4 teaspoon ground cinnamon
- 1/4 teaspoon ground ginger
- 3 tablespoons brown sugar or honey
- 1 cup orange juice
- 3 tablespoons flour mixed with 2 tablespoons cold water

PREPARATION

1. Place all ingredients, except flour and water mixture, in the slow cooker or Crock Pot. Cover and cook on low 6 to 7 hours, until chicken is tender. Add flour mixture in the last 15 to 20 minutes and cook until thickened. Taste and adjust seasonings.
2. Serves 4.

Chicken with Dressing and Gravy, Slow Cooker

INGREDIENTS

- 1 package (6 ounces) seasoned stuffing crumbs (a "stove top" type stuffing mix)
- 1 large potato, cut in small dice
- 1 bunch green onions, chopped
- 2 ribs celery, chopped
- 1/2 cup water
- 3 tablespoons butter, divided
- 1 teaspoon poultry seasoning, divided
- 1 to 1 1/2 pounds chicken tenderloins or boneless breasts
- 1 jar (12 ounces) chicken gravy, such as Heinz Homestyle Chicken Gravy

PREPARATION

1. In a lightly buttered or sprayed crockpot, toss stuffing crumbs with diced potato, green onion, celery, 2 tablespoons melted butter and 1/2 cup water. Sprinkle with about 1/2 teaspoon of poultry seasoning. Top stuffing with chicken pieces; drizzle with remaining butter and poultry seasoning. Pour gravy over chicken. Cover and cook on low for 6 to 7 hours.

Chicken with Macaroni and Smoked Gouda Cheese

INGREDIENTS

- 1 1/2 pounds chicken tenders, boneless
- 2 small zucchini, halved and sliced 1/8-inch thick
- 1 package chicken gravy mix (approx. 1 oz)
- 2 tablespoons water
- salt and pepper to taste
- pinch of ground nutmeg, fresh if possible
- 8 ounces smoked Gouda cheese, grated
- 2 tablespoons evaporated milk or light cream
- 1 large tomato, chopped
- 4 cups cooked macaroni or small shell pasta

PREPARATION

1. Cut chicken into 1-inch cubes; place in crockpot. Add zucchini, gravy mix, water, and seasoning. Cover and cook for 5 to 6 hours on low. Add smoked gouda cheese, milk or cream, and chopped tomato to the crockpot during the last 20 minutes, or while the macaroni is cooking. Stir in hot cooked macaroni.
2. Chicken recipe serves 4.

Chicken With Pearl Onions and Mushrooms, Slow Cooker

INGREDIENTS

- 4 to 6 boneless chicken breast halves, cut in 1-inch chunks

- 1 can (10 3/4 ounces) cream of chicken or cream of chicken and mushroom soup

- 8 ounces sliced mushrooms

- 1 bag (16 ounces) frozen pearl onions

- salt and pepper, to taste

- parsley, chopped, for garnish

PREPARATION

1. Wash chicken and pat dry. Cut into chunks about 1/2 to 1-inch and put in a large bowl. Add the soup, mushrooms, and onions; stir to combine. Spray the slow cooker insert with cooking spray.
2. Spoon the chicken mixture into the crockpot and sprinkle with salt and pepper.
3. Cover and cook on LOW for 6 to 8 hours, stirring about halfway through the cooking time, if possible.
4. Garnish with fresh chopped parsley, if desired, and serve over hot cooked rice or with potatoes.
5. Serves 4 to 6.

Chicken With Pineapple

INGREDIENTS

- 1 to 1 1/2 pounds chicken tenders, cut in 1-inch pieces
- 2/3 cup pineapple preserves
- 1 tablespoon plus 1 teaspoon teriyaki sauce
- 2 cloves garlic sliced thinly
- 1 tablespoon dried minced onion (or 1 bunch fresh green onions, chopped)
- 1 tablespoon lemon juice
- 1/2 teaspoon ground ginger
- dash cayenne, to taste
- 1 package (10 oz) sugar snap peas, thawed

PREPARATION

1. Place chicken pieces in slow cooker/Crock Pot.
2. Combine preserves, teriyaki sauce, garlic, onion, lemon juice, ginger, and cayenne; stir well. Spoon over chicken, toss to coat.
3. Cover and cook on low 6 to 7 hours. Add peas last 30 minutes.
4. Serves 4.

Country Captain Chicken

INGREDIENTS

-
- 2 medium-size Granny Smith apples, cored and diced (unpeeled)
-
- 1/4 cup finely chopped onion
-
- 1 small green bell pepper, seeded and finely chopped
-
- 3 cloves garlic, minced
-
- 2 tablespoons raisins or currants
-
- 2 to 3 teaspoons curry powder
-
- 1 teaspoon ground ginger
-
- 1/4 teaspoon ground red pepper, or to taste
-
- 1 can (about 14 1/2 oz.) diced tomatoes
-
- 6 boneless chicken breast halves, skin removed
-
- 1/2 cup chicken broth
-
- 1 cup long-grain converted white rice

- 1 pound medium to large shrimp, shelled and deveined, uncooked, optional

- 1/3 cup slivered almonds

- kosher salt

- Chopped parsley

PREPARATION

1. In a 4- to 6-quart slow cooker, combine diced apples, onion, bell pepper, garlic, golden raisins or currants, curry powder, ginger, and ground red pepper; stir in tomatoes.
2. Arrange the chicken over the tomato mixture, overlapping pieces slightly. Pour chicken broth over the chicken breast halves. Cover and cook on LOW until chicken is very tender when pierced with a fork, about 4 to 6 hours.
3. Remove chicken to a warm plate, cover lightly, and keep warm in a 200° F oven or warming drawer.
4. Stir the rice into cooking liquid. Increase temperature to high; cover and cook, stirring once or twice, until rice is almost tender, about 35 minutes. Stir in shrimp, if using; cover and cook for about 15 minutes longer, until shrimp are opaque in center; cut to test.
5. Meanwhile, toast almonds in a small nonstick frying pan over medium heat until golden brown, stirring occasionally. Set aside.
6. To serve the dish, season rice mixture to taste with salt. Mound in a warm serving dish; arrange chicken on top. Sprinkle with parsley and almonds.

Country Chicken and Mushrooms

INGREDIENTS

- 1 jar country gravy

- 4 to 6 chicken breasts

- 8 ounces sliced mushrooms

- salt and pepper to taste

PREPARATION

1. Combine all ingredients; cover and cook on low for 6 to 7 hours. Serve with rice or noodles.
2. Serves 4 to 6.

Cranberry Chicken

INGREDIENTS

- 2 pounds boneless chicken breasts, skin removed
- 1/2 cup chopped onion
- 2 teaspoons vegetable oil
- 2 teaspoons salt
- 1/2 teaspoon ground cinnamon
- 1/4 teaspoon ground ginger
- 1/8 teaspoon ground nutmeg
- dash ground allspice
- 1 cup orange juice
- 2 teaspoons finely grated orange peel
- 2 cups fresh or frozen cranberries
- 1/4 cup brown sugar

PREPARATION

1. Brown chicken pieces and onion in oil; sprinkle with salt.
2. Add browned chicken, onions and other ingredients to crock pot.
3. Cover and cook on LOW 5 1/2 to 7 hours.
4. If desired, thicken juices near the end of cooking time with a mixture of about 2 tablespoons cornstarch combined with 2 tablespoons cold water.

Creamy Italian Chicken

INGREDIENTS

- 4 boneless skinless chicken breast halves
- 1 envelope Italian salad dressing mix
- 1/3 cup water
- 1 package (8 ozs.) cream cheese, softened
- 1 can (10 3/4 ozs.) condensed cream of chicken soup, undiluted
- 1 can (4 ozs.) mushroom stems and pieces, drained
- Hot cooked rice or noodles

PREPARATION

1. Place the chicken breast halves in a slow cooker. Combine salad dressing mix and water; pour over chicken. Cover and cook on LOW for 3 hours. In a small mixing bowl, whisk together cream cheese and soup until blended. Stir in mushrooms. Pour cream cheese mixture over chicken. Cook 1 to 3 hours longer or until chicken juices run clear. Serve Italian chicken with rice or hot cooked noodles.
2. Serves 4.

Crockpot Korean Short Rib Tacos

Ingredients

Ribs:

- 10 cloves garlic, minced
- inches of fresh ginger, peeled and minced
- 1/2 c. soy sauce
- + 6 tbsp. brown sugar
- 3/4 c. rice vinegar (also called rice wine vinegar)
- tbsp. sesame oil
- tsp. red pepper flakes
- lbs. beef ribs (could be called short ribs or back ribs also)

Slaw:

- 2 tsp. rice vinegar

- tsp. sugar

- pinches salt

- 1/2 of a large onion - very thinly sliced

- large carrots, peeled then "sliced" into long thin strips with your peeler

- pinch red pepper flakes

- handful cilantro, chopped

- tsp. or drizzle sesame oil

- sqeeze lime juice (about 1 tsp.)

- tsp. fresh ginger, FINELY minced

- 1/4 c. toasted sesame seeds

Instructions

For the Ribs

1.
Mix garlic, ginger, soy sauce, brown sugar, rice vinegar, sesame oil, and red pepper flakes.

2.
Place ribs in a greased crockpot and pour sauce over ribs. Turn crock pot on low heat. Cover with a lid and cook for 6-8 hours, moving the ribs around 2 or 3 times so that they all get a turn being immersed in the sauce.

3.
When the time is up and meat is fork tender, remove meat from pot, discard bones. Place meat in the fridge to chill to touch.

4.
Meanwhile, skim fat off the top of the sauce. Place sauce in a pan and simmer until thickened (about 25 mins.)

5.
Once meat is cool to touch, pull apart with your fingers or with 2 forks. Pour some sauce back into the meat and reheat (you can use your crockpot on high for about 20 mins. or your microwave). You can serve the extra sauce on the side (goes especially well with rice recipe included).

For the Slaw

1.
(To toast the sesame seeds, heat a small pan over medium heat. Add the sesame seeds and stir for about 4 mins. until golden brown and aromatic. Remove immediately and set aside.)

2.
In a small bowl, mix together the vinegar, sugar, and salt. Add the sliced onions to the mixture and let sit for about 15 mins. to pickle & sweeten the onions.

3.

Pour onions & mixture into a medium bowl. Add carrot pieces. Gently stir in your red pepper flakes, cilantro, sesame oil, lime juice, and ginger.

4.

Reserve toasted sesame seeds until JUST before serving so they retain their crunch. Can be made a few hours ahead of time and kept in the fridge, sans sesame seeds.

5.

(Optional Rice: we served this with the tacos to make the meal a little more filling)

In a pot, heat the oil over medium heat. Saute garlic, ginger, and onions for 3-5 minutes or until starting to soften. Add rice, stir to toast the rice for about 2 more minutes. Add the water. Bring the mixture to boiling. Reduce heat. Cover and simmer for about 45 minutes until water is absorbed and rice is tender. Stir in soy sauce and lime juice to taste.

Provencal Chicken and Beans

Ingredients

24 oz boneless, skinless chicken breast

1 yellow bell pepper, diced

1 red bell pepper, diced

1 (16 oz) can cannellini beans, drained and rinsed

1 (14.5 oz) can petite diced tomatoes with basil and oregano or any style of canned tomatoes

1 dash salt

1 dash black pepper

2 t dried basil

1 t dried thyme

Directions

Place all ingredients into a slow cooker, stir and cover with lid; cook on low heat for 7 hours. If you are running late, the mixture will hold for 8 hours, so don't rush.

Buffalo Chicken Sandwiches (Made in the Crockpot)

3 boneless skinless chicken breasts

1, 12 oz bottle of Franks Red Hot Buffalo Sauce

3 tablespoons 0% Greek Yogurt

Directions

1. Place the chicken (seasoned with salt and pepper or herbs of choice) in crock pot. Pour the bottle of wing sauce on top of the chicken. Cook on low for 7-9 or on high for 4-6 hours. I cooked mine for 5 on high and it was still perfect.

2. Remove chicken and shred it using two forks. Before returning the chicken to the sauce added 3 table spoons of greek yogurt and whisk. Return shredded chicken and mix. Serve on a bun or bread or wrap or cracker!

Slow Cooker Spicy Barbecued Chicken

Ingredients

- 8 drumsticks, skin removed (optional, 3 split breasts or 6 thighs)

- Barbecue Sauce

- 1 tablespoon canola oil

- 1 sweet onion, finely diced

- 1 clove garlic, minced

- 1 (8 ounce) can tomato sauce

- 1/4 cup honey

- 1/4 cup balsamic vinegar (use white balsamic vinegar for gluten free)

- 1 teaspoon Dijon mustard

- 1 tablespoon Red Hot Sauce, 'Frank's Red Hot' was used in this recipe

- 1/2 teaspoon cayenne pepper

- 2 teaspoons chili powder
- Sea Salt to taste
- Spice Rub
- 1 teaspoon chipotle chile pepper
- 1 teaspoon dried oregano
- 1 teaspoon cumin
- 1 teaspoon chili powder
- 1 teaspoon ground mustard
- 1 teaspoon paprika
- 1 teaspoon black pepper
- 1 teaspoon cayenne pepper
- Sea Salt to taste

Directions

In a medium sauce pan add canola oil, turn to medium-low heat and saute onion and garlic until tender, about 5 minutes. Add the remaining barbecue sauce ingredients, stir and simmer until sauce has thickened, about 30 minutes. While the sauce is cooking down, combine spice rub and coat all sides of drumsticks.

After sauce has cooked down and thickened, place drumsticks in the slow cooker, pour barbecue sauce over and ensure all drumsticks are covered. Cover, turn to high and cook approximately 3 hours or until cooked through. Or, turn slow cooker to low and cook

Slow Cooker Salsa Chicken

Ingredients

2 pounds (32 ounces) chicken breasts, boneless and skinless

1 cup salsa, homemade or purchased

1 cup petite diced canned tomatoes (choose low-sodium)

2 tablespoons Taco Seasoning

1 cup onions, diced fine

1/2 cup celery diced fine

1/2 cup carrots, shredded

3 tablespoons sour cream, reduced fat

Directions

Place the chicken in a slow cooker. Sprinkle the taco seasoning over the meat then layer the vegetables and salsa on top. Pour a half cup water over the mixture, set on low and cook for 6-8 hours. The meat is cooked when it shreds or reaches an internal temperature of 165°F. When ready to serve, break up the chicken with two forks then stir in the sour cream.

Makes eight 1 cup servings.

Pulled Pork with Caramelized Onions

Ingredients

- 1 tablespoon extra-virgin olive oil

- 3 large onions, thinly sliced

- 1/3 cup raw cane sugar, such as Demerara or turbinado (see Notes)

- 4 cloves garlic, minced

- 1 teaspoon dried oregano

- 1 teaspoon freshly ground pepper

- 1/2 teaspoon salt

- 1/3 cup cider vinegar

- 1 cup chili sauce, such as Heinz

- 1 1/2-3 teaspoons minced chipotle chile in adobo sauce (see Notes)

- 3 pounds boneless pork shoulder or blade (butt) roast, trimmed

Directions

Heat oil in a large skillet over medium-high heat. Add onions and cook, stirring occasionally, until they begin to soften, 3 to 6 minutes. Add sugar and continue to cook, stirring constantly, until the onions are golden brown, 6 to 8 minutes more. Add garlic, oregano, pepper and salt and cook, stirring, for 1 minute. Add vinegar and bring to a boil. Cook until mostly evaporated, 30 seconds to 1 minute. Remove from the heat and stir in chili sauce and chipotle to taste.

Place pork in a 4-quart (or larger) slow cooker and cover with the sauce. Cover and cook until the pork is almost falling apart, about 4 hours on High or 8 hours on Low.

Transfer the pork to a cutting board and shred using two forks. Stir back into the sauce.

Slow Cooker Marinara Chicken and Vegetables

Ingredients

2 pounds boneless, skinless chicken breasts

4 cloves garlic, peeled and crushed

4 tomatoes, chopped or one 14.5-ounce can low-sodium tomatoes, drained

4 medium ribs celery, diced (1 cup)

2 small zucchini, diced (2 cups)

1 bell pepper, cored, seeded, and diced

One 18-ounce jar low-sodium marinara sauce

1 tsp dried basil

1 tsp dried thyme

Directions

Place the chicken in the slow cooker; add the garlic, tomatoes, celery, zucchini, and pepper.

Pour the marinara sauce over all, and sprinkle the basil and thyme on top.

Set the slow cooker on low and cook for 6 to 7 hours. Before serving, shred the chicken

with a fork.

Slow Cooker Lemon Chicken

Ingredients

- 12 boneless, skinless chicken thighs
- Kosher or sea salt to taste
- ¾ teaspoon pepper, divided
- 2 tablespoons olive oil, divided
- 1 lemon, sliced (optional)
- 1 cup chicken broth (fat free, low sodium)
- 3 tablespoons freshly squeezed lemon juice
- ¼ cup flour, optional corn starch
- ½ teaspoon ground cumin
- ¾ cup pitted green olives

Directions

Sprinkle chicken thighs evenly with salt and ½ teaspoon pepper.

Heat 1 tablespoon oil in a large skillet over medium-high heat; add half of chicken. Cook about 3 minutes per side, or until browned. Transfer to a slow cooker. Add remaining 1 tablespoon olive oil to skillet, and repeat procedure with remaining chicken.

Combine broth, juice, flour and cumin, stirring with a whisk. Pour broth mixture over chicken.

Top with olives and remaining ¼ teaspoon pepper. Cover and cook on low heat for 6 hours. Add lemon slices as a garnish to serve, if using.

Vegetarian Chili Ole! Recipe

Ingredients

- 1 can (16 ounces) kidney beans, rinsed and drained
- 1 can (15 ounces) black beans, rinsed and drained
- 1 can (14-1/2 ounces) diced tomatoes, undrained
- 1-1/2 cups frozen corn
- 1 large onion, chopped
- 1 medium zucchini, chopped
- 1 medium sweet red pepper, chopped
- 1 can (4 ounces) chopped green chilies
- 1 ounce Mexican chocolate, chopped
- 1 cup water
- 1 can (6 ounces) tomato paste

- 1 tablespoon cornmeal

- 1 tablespoon chili powder

- 1/2 teaspoon salt

- 1/2 teaspoon dried oregano

- 1/2 teaspoon ground cumin

- 1/4 teaspoon hot pepper sauce, optional

- Optional toppings: diced tomatoes, chopped green onions and crumbled queso fresco

Directions

In a 4-qt. slow cooker, combine the first nine ingredients. Combine the water, tomato paste, cornmeal, chili powder, salt, oregano, cumin and pepper sauce if desired until smooth; stir into slow cooker. Cover and cook on low for 6-8 hours or until vegetables are tender.

Serve with toppings of your choice.

Char Siu Pork Roast

Ingredients

- 1/4 cup lower-sodium soy sauce
- 1/4 cup hoisin sauce
- 3 tablespoons ketchup
- 3 tablespoons honey
- 2 teaspoons minced garlic
- 2 teaspoons grated peeled fresh ginger
- 1 teaspoon dark sesame oil
- 1/2 teaspoon five-spice powder
- 1 (2-pound) boneless pork shoulder (Boston butt), trimmed
- 1/2 cup fat-free, lower-sodium chicken broth

Preparation

Combine first 8 ingredients in a small bowl, stirring well with a whisk. Place in a large zip-top plastic bag. Add pork to bag; seal. Marinate in refrigerator at least 2 hours, turning occasionally.

Place pork and marinade in an electric slow cooker. Cover and cook on low for 8 hours.

Remove pork from slow cooker using a slotted spoon; place on a cutting board or work surface. Cover with aluminum foil; keep warm.

Add broth to sauce in slow cooker. Cover and cook on low for 30 minutes or until sauce thickens. Shred pork with 2 forks; serve with sauce.

Thyme-Scented White Bean Cassoulet

Ingredients

- 1 tablespoon olive oil

- 1 1/2 cups chopped onion $

- 1 1/2 cups (1/2-inch-thick) slices diagonally cut carrot $

- 1 cup (1/2-inch-thick) slices diagonally cut parsnip

- 2 garlic cloves, minced

- 3 cups cooked Great Northern beans

- 3/4 cup organic vegetable broth

- 1/2 teaspoon dried thyme

- 1/4 teaspoon salt

- 1/4 teaspoon freshly ground black pepper

- 1 (28-ounce) can diced tomatoes, undrained

- 1 bay leaf

- 1/4 cup dry breadcrumbs

- 1 ounce grated fresh Parmesan cheese (about 1/4 cup)

- 2 tablespoons butter, melted $

- 2 links frozen meatless Italian sausage, thawed and chopped

- 2 tablespoons chopped fresh parsley

Preparation

Heat oil in a large nonstick skillet over medium heat. Add onion, carrot, parsnip, and garlic; cover and cook 5 minutes or until tender.

Place in a 5-quart electric slow cooker. Add beans and next 6 ingredients (through bay leaf). Cover and cook on low 8 hours or until vegetables are tender.

Combine breadcrumbs, cheese, and butter in a small bowl; toss with a fork until moist. Stir breadcrumb mixture and sausage into bean mixture; sprinkle with parsley.

Vegetable and Chickpea Curry

Makes: 4 to 6 servings

Ingredients

3 cups cauliflower florets

1 15-ounce can chickpeas, rinsed and drained

1 cup loose-pack frozen cut green beans

1 cup sliced carrots

1/2 cup chopped onion

1 14-ounce can vegetable broth

2-3 teaspoons curry powder

1 14-ounce can light coconut milk

1/4 cup shredded fresh basil leaves

Cooked brown rice (optional)

Directions

In a 3-1/2- or 4-quart slow cooker, combine cauliflower, chickpeas, green beans, carrots, and onion. Stir in broth and curry powder.

Cover and cook on low-heat setting for 5 to 6 hours or on high-heat setting for 2 1/2 to 3 hours.

Stir in coconut milk and shredded basil leaves. Spoon rice, if using, into bowls, and ladle curry over the top.

Nutrition facts per serving: 219 calories, 8g protein, 32g carbohydrate, 7g fat (4g saturated), 9g fiber

Slow Cooker Steak Fajitas

Ingredients

- 1 ½ lbs flank steak, preferably grass fed (we buy ours from Baucom's Best at the Matthews Farmers' Market)
- 1 ½ teaspoons chili powder
- 1 teaspoon cumin
- 1 teaspoon coriander
- ½ teaspoon salt
- ¼ teaspoon black pepper
- 2 tablespoons soy sauce, preferably the low-sodium variety
- 1 jalapeno pepper, seeded and chopped
- 2 cloves garlic, minced
- 4 – 5 bell peppers, any color
- 1 onion

Directions

1. Mix together the dry spices with a fork including the chili powder, cumin, coriander, salt and pepper.
2. Rub the spice mixture over all sides of the flank steak and place it in the bottom of the slow cooker. Sprinkle the soy sauce on top.
3. Top the flank steak with the diced jalapeno and minced garlic. Slice the bell peppers and onion and throw those on top of the steak as well.
4. Turn the slow cooker onto HIGH and cook for 5 – 6 hours or until the steak can easily be shredded with two forks.
5. Drain the meat and peppers well then serve.

Best Whole Chicken in a Crockpot

Ingredients

- 2 teaspoons paprika
- 1 teaspoon salt
- 1 teaspoon onion powder
- 1 teaspoon thyme
- ½ teaspoon garlic powder
- ¼ teaspoon cayenne (red) pepper
- ¼ teaspoon black pepper
- 1 onion
- 1 large chicken

Instructions

1. Combine the dried spices in a small bowl.
2. Loosely chop the onion and place it in the bottom of the slow cooker.
3. Remove any giblets from the chicken and then rub the spice mixture all over. You can even put some of the spices inside the cavity and under the skin covering the breasts.
4. Put prepared chicken on top of the onions in the slow cooker, cover it, and turn it on to high.
5. There is no need to add any liquid.
6. Cook for 4 – 5 hours on high (for a 3 or 4 pound chicken) or until the chicken is falling off the bone. Don't forget to make your homemade stock with the leftover bones!

Thai Pork with Peanut Sauce

Ingredients

- One(2 pound) boneless pork loin, fat trimmed and cut into 4 pieces
- 2 red bell peppers, cut into strips
- 1/2 cup prepared teriyaki sauce (I use Soy Vay brand)
- 2 T rice vinegar
- 1 t red pepper flakes
- 3 cloves garlic
- 2-3 T creamy peanut butter

Possible garnishes

- Chopped green onions (about 1/2 cup)
- roasted chop peanuts (about 1/4 cup)
- 1 lime sliced into wedges

Directions

1. Spray slow cooker with cooking spray. Place all ingredients except for peanut butter and garnishes in the slow cooker.
2. Cook on low for 8-9 hours.
3. Before serving, remove pork and cut up. Mix peanut butter with sauce in slow cooker until peanut butter dissolves.
4. Toss pork back in slow cooker and coat with sauce. Serve over rice with garnishes!

Slow Cooker Apple Cider Pork Roast

Ingredients

- 4 lb. pork, shoulder roast, boneless

- salt to taste

- freshly ground black pepper to taste

- 1 T. vegetable oil

- 2 shallots, sliced

- 1 celery, rib, chopped

- 1/2 c. apple cider vinegar

- 2 1/2 c. apple cider

- 4 cloves garlic, peeled

- 1 bay leaf

- 1 1/2 tsp. Dijon mustard

- 1 pinch cayenne pepper, or more for your taste

- 2 T. butter, cold, cut into small pieces

- 1 T. herbs, chopped fresh, Italian parsley, sage, or thyme

Directions

1.
Season pork roast with salt and black pepper.

2.
Heat oil in a large skillet over high heat. Searing pork on all sides in the hot oil until browned, about 3 minutes per side.

3.
Transfer roast to the slow cooker.

4.
Reduce heat to medium heat for the skillet.

5.
Cook and stir shallots and celery in the skillet until they begin to soften, about 4 minutes.

6.
Pour in apple cider vinegar and cook, scraping up any browned bits, until liquid is nearly evaporated, 4 to 5 minutes longer.

7.
Place the shallot mixture over pork roast in the crock pot. Adding apple cider, garlic cloves, and bay leaf.

8. Cover. Cook on Low, until roast is fork-tender but not falling apart, about 6 hours. Turning the pork roast every 1 to 2 hours.

9. Transfer the pork roast to a plate and cover loosely with foil.

10. Pour remaining liquid from the slow cooker through a fine mesh strainer into a large saucepan; place over high heat.

11. Discard bay leaf and other solids.

12. Bring sauce mixture to a boil, decrease heat and cook, skimming fat from the top, until reduced to 1/4 of the original volume, about 10 minutes.

13. Remove mixture from heat and stir in Dijon mustard and cayenne pepper.

14. Whisk slowly the cold butter into above mixture until incorporated.

15. Sprinkle in fresh herbs and season with salt and black pepper to taste.

Slow Cooker Ham & White Beans

- 1 lb package dried northern beans

- ham bone, hocks, shanks or diced ham (about 1 pound)

- 2 tsp onion powder

- 6 cups water

- salt & pepper to taste

Instructions

1. Rinse and sort the beans for any pebbles. Add the the rinsed beans, onion powder, salt, pepper, and ham to the crock pot. Add water. Cover and cook on low about 8 hours, until beans are tender. Remove ham bone, shanks or hocks and pull off the meat. Add meat to the crock pot and mix. Serve with cornbread.

Slow Cooker Cilantro Lime Chicken

Ingredients:

- 24-oz. jar medium salsa

- Juice from one lime

- 1/4 cup fresh cilantro, chopped

- 1.25-oz. package taco seasoning

- 2 jalapeños peppers, finely chopped (optional)

- 6 boneless chicken breast halves, defrosted

Directions

1.
In a slow cooker, mix together the salsa, lime juice, cilantro, taco seasoning and jalapenos. Add the chicken and coat with the salsa mixture.

2.
Allow the chicken to cook, covered, in the slow cooker on Low setting for 6 hours. Serve chicken with salsa mixture spooned over top, or shred and use as a taco filling.

Pesto Lasagna with Spinach and Mushrooms

Ingredients

- 4 cups torn spinach
- 2 cups sliced cremini mushrooms
- 1/2 cup commercial pesto
- 3/4 cup (3 ounces) shredded part-skim mozzarella cheese
- 3/4 cup (3 ounces) shredded provolone cheese
- 1 (15-ounce) carton fat-free ricotta cheese
- 1 large egg, lightly beaten $
- 3/4 cup (3 ounces) grated fresh Parmesan cheese, divided
- 1 (25.5-ounce) bottle fat-free tomato-basil pasta sauce
- 1 (8-ounce) can tomato sauce
- Cooking spray
- 1 (8-ounce) package precooked lasagna noodles (12 noodles)

Preparation

1. Arrange the spinach in a vegetable steamer; steam, covered, 3 minutes or until spinach wilts. Drain, squeeze dry, and coarsely chop. Combine spinach, mushrooms, and pesto in a medium bowl, stirring to combine; set aside.
2. Combine mozzarella, provolone, ricotta, and beaten egg in a medium bowl, stirring well to combine. Stir in 1/4 cup

Parmesan, and set aside. Combine the pasta sauce and the tomato sauce in a medium bowl.
3. Spread 1 cup pasta sauce mixture in the bottom of a 6-quart oval electric slow cooker coated with cooking spray. Arrange 3 noodles over pasta sauce mixture; top with 1 cup cheese mixture and 1 cup spinach mixture. Repeat the layers, ending with spinach mixture.
4. Arrange 3 noodles over spinach mixture; top with remaining 1 cup cheese mixture and 1 cup pasta sauce mixture. Place remaining 3 noodles over sauce mixture; spread remaining sauce mixture over noodles. Sprinkle with the remaining 1/2 cup Parmesan. Cover with lid; cook on LOW 5 hours or until done.

Crock Pot Tuscan Chicken & Beans

Ingredients

- 4 boneless, skinless chicken breasts
- 1 can fire roasted tomatoes, with sauce
- 1 can white beans, drained and rinsed
- 1 bell pepper, chopped
- 1 tsp dried basil

Method

1. Place chicken in crock pot and sprinkle with basil.
2. Place bell peppers, beans and tomatoes over the chicken evenly.
3. Cook on low for 6-8 hours.
4. Serve with pasta or rice.

Crockpot Pineapple Chicken

Ingredients

- 3-4 Chicken Breasts (about 2 lbs)

- 1 can of pineapple in juice (tidbits, chucks, rings, it doesn't matter)

- 1 medium onion

- 2 TBSP soy sauce

- ½ cup chicken broth

Directions

1.
Chop onion and place in crock pot.

2.
Place Chicken Breast on top of onion.

3.
Dump the can of pineapple (juice and all) over the chicken.

4.
Dump the soy sauce and the chicken broth on top of everything.

5.
Cover and cook on HIGH in the crockpot for 4-5 hours or on low for 6-8 h.

6.
Serve over rice and with a steamed veggie.

Skinny Chicken Enchilads

Author: Pinch of Yum

Ingredients

- 1 lb. chicken breasts

- 1 can black beans, drained and rinsed

- 1 can corn, drained

- 16 oz. fresh salsa

- 3 tablespoons taco seasoning

- ¼ cup water (optional)

- 12 small corn tortillas

- 1 cup shredded cheddar cheese

- 1 avocado, diced

- ¼ cup crema (see notes)

- fresh cilantro, Cotija cheese for topping

Directions

1.

Put the first 6 ingredients in a crockpot. If your salsa is not very saucy, be sure to include the ¼ cup water or more if necessary. Cook on high for about 3 hours (or longer on the low setting) until chicken is cooked through. You can also cut the chicken breasts into halves to help them cook faster. Use 2 forks to shred the chicken and mix everything together.

2.

Preheat the oven to 400 degrees. Soften the corn tortillas in the microwave, 3 at a time, for about 25 seconds. Fill them with a few tablespoons of filling, roll once, and place seam-side down in a large baking dish (I did 2 smaller baking dishes). Continue until all tortillas have been filled, rolled and placed in dish. Be sure to pack them in tightly next to each other so that they don't come apart.

3.

Sprinkle evenly with the shredded cheese and bake for about 15-20 minutes, until cheese is melted and bubbly and everything is heated through.

4.

Remove from oven and drizzle with crema. Sprinkle with avocado pieces, fresh cilantro, and Cotija cheese crumbles.

Balsamic Roast Beef Recipe

Ingredients

- 1 3-4 pound boneless roast beef (chuck or round roast)
- 1 cup beef broth
- ½ cup balsamic vinegar
- 1 tablespoon Worcestershire sauce
- 1 tablespoon soy sauce
- 1 tablespoon honey
- ½ teaspoon red pepper flakes
- 4 cloves garlic, chopped

Directions

1. Place roast beef into the insert of your slow cooker. In a 2-cup measuring cup, mix together all remaining ingredients. Pour over roast beef and set the timer for your slow cooker. (4 hours on High or 6-8 hours on Low)

2.
Once roast beef has cooked, remove from slow cooker with tongs into a serving dish. Break apart lightly with two forks and then ladle about ¼ - ½ cup of gravy over roast beef.

3.
Store remaining gravy in an airtight container in the refrigerator for another use.

Italian Stallion Crockpot Chicken

Ingredients

- 3-4 lbs of boneless, skinless chicken breasts
- 5 medium tomatoes
- 3/4 cup chopped onion (we use Vidalia/Sweet)
- 3 Tbsp minced garlic
- 2 Tbsp tomato paste
- 2 Tbsp olive oil
- 1 Tbsp honey

Dry Ingredients/Spices

- 1 Tbsp basil
- 1 Tbsp thyme
- 1 Tbsp red pepper flakes
- 1 Tbsp oregano
- 1 tsp rosemary
- 1 tsp parsley
- 1 tsp sea salt
- 1 tsp black pepper
- 1 tsp bay leaves

Directions

1. Mix all ingredients (not including the chicken breasts) together in a blender/food processor (must hold at least 5 cups - we use a Vitamix) and blend for about 30 seconds until ingredients are mixed well.
2. Place blended pasta sauce in sauce pan and simmer on low/medium heat for about 10-15 minutes until sauce takes on a thicker consistency and a dark shade of red.
3. Mix chicken breasts and pasta sauce in crock pot and cook on low heat for at least 7 hours.
4. After 7 hours, you will notice the sauce looks very runny, this is normal. Remove crock pot from heating base, shred chicken with a wooden spoon or spatula and as it cools, the shredded chicken will absorb the juices from the pasta sauce.

Ginger Cranberry Pork Roast

Ingredients

- 3 pounds pork roasts

- 2 12-ounce package fresh cranberries or 2 cans of whole cranberries

- 1 cup peeled and sliced or minced ginger

- 2 tablespoons rapadura sugar (if using canned cranberries, or to taste...more sugar is needed for fresh cranberries)

- 2 tablespoons of arrowroot flour (or any thinkening agent of your choice)

- 1 cup filtered water

Instructions

1.
Dump all ingredients (except water) into one, one gallon bag.

2.
Label and put in freezer

3.
Day of cooking dump contents of bag into slow cooker, add the water

4.
Cook on low for 4 to 6 hours, or until fully cooked

Remember each slow cooker is different, so the first time you make a recipe, really watch it so you don't over or under cook it.

Serve with sauteed broccoli in lots of butter. I cook frozen broccoli this way, no need to thaw, just dump frozen broccoli into a hot pan with hot butter and it is delicious.

Pot Roast in the Crock Pot

Ingredients:

- 1 (2 1/2-3 lb) beef roast, cut to fit pot or crock pot (chuck, shoulder or round)

- 2 tablespoons oil

- salt and pepper , to taste

- 1 tablespoon Worcestershire Sauce

- 1 teaspoon basil crushed

- 5-6 new potatoes or 2 medium sweet potatoes

- 1/2 bag baby carrots

- 1 onion, cut into wedges

- 2 celery stalks, bias-cut in 1-inch pieces (I didn't have any)

- 1/4 cup flour

- 1/2 cup red wine or 1/2 cup beef broth

- 1/2 cup water

Directions:

1.
Carrots, potatoes, and onions in the bottom of the crock pot.

2.
Trim fat from meat. Brown meat on all sides in hot oil in a skillet. Drain fat. Place meat on top of the veggies in the crock pot.

3.
Make Sauce. Mix 3/4 cup water, Worcestershire sauce, red wine, basil and salt and pepper to taste.

4.
Pour over roast.

5.
Cook pot roast, covered on low for 10-12 hours or high for 5-6 hours.

6.
Make gravy when ready. In a small bowl, stir 1/2 cup water into flour. Stir into pan juices. Cook, stirring, on medium heat until thickened, then 1 minute more. Season to taste. Serve with pot roast.

Coconut Almond Cranberry Chicken

Ingredients

- 1/2 cup almonds, chopped

- 1 (15 ounce) can light coconut milk

- 1/2 cup dried cranberries (I used fruit juice sweetened cranberries from Whole Foods)

- 4 cups raw spinach leaves, tightly packed when measuring

- 4 chicken breasts (about 7 ounces each), chopped into bite-sized pieces

- 1/2 teaspoon finely grated fresh ginger (grate on a microplane for best results)

- 1/2 teaspoon cinnamon

Directions

1. Combine all ingredients in a large pan and cook over medium to medium-high until the chicken is fully cooked through. Serve by itself or over brown rice or whole grain pasta.

Crock Pot Orange Chicken

Ingredients

- 4 boneless skinless chicken breasts, chopped into cubes
- 1 cup of real orange juice, no additives
- 1/4 cup of honey
- 1 tsp marjoram
- 2 small oranges or cuties
- 1 TBS wheat flour, optional
- 1 TBS soy sauce, optional

Instructions

1. Add the chicken breasts to the crock pot.
2. Mix the other ingredients together and pour over the chicken.

3.
Cook on low for 6 hours or high for 3.

4.
Open the pot and stir. I added the flour to thicken it a little but you don't have to.

5.
Open the orange and add the segments into the pot and stir.

6.
Cook for a further 15 minutes.

7.
Serve over rice, couscous or quinoa.

Turkey Pad Thai Recipe

Ingredients

- 1/2 C hot water
- 1/4 C raw sugar
- 2 T rice vinegar
- 2 T low sodium soy sauce
- 1 T chili garlic sauce
- 1 lime, juiced
- 2 C leftover turkey, cubed
- 2 C broccoli slaw, packed
- 1 C bok choy, chopped and packed
- 1 C napa cabbage, chopped and packed
- 1/2 C cilantro packed
- 1/2 med. onion, sliced
- 3 garlic cloves, minced
- 3 scallions, chopped
- 8 oz. whole wheat organic linguine

Directions

1. Combine water, sugar, vinegar, garlic sauce and lime juice in a slow cooker and stir to dissolve sugar
2. Stir turkey in to sauce to cover

3. Add broccoli slaw, bok choy, cabbage, cilantro, onion, garlic and scallions and stir to mix
4. Cook on low for 6 hours or high for 3 hours
5. Make linguini as per package directions just before serving
6. Toss with slow cooker mixture
7. Serve and Enjoy!

Turkey Lasagna

Ingredients

- 1 lb ground extra lean turkey (454 g)
- 1.5 cups fresh mushrooms, sliced
- 1 cup onion, chopped
- 1 28 oz can diced tomatoes, no salt added, drained
- 2 Tbsp tomato paste
- 1 tsp garlic powder
- 1 tsp dried oregano
- 1 tsp dried basil
- 2 cups spinach leaves
- 1 cup cottage cheese
- 1 egg, beaten
- 3/4 cup low fat Italian cheese blend
- 9 whole grain lasagna noodles

Directions

If your using regular lasagna noodles (not the oven ready kind), submerge the noodles in cold water while prepping the ingredients. It will soften them.

Spray crock pot with cooking spray. In a bowl, combine diced tomatoes, tomato paste, oregano, garlic powder & basil. In a small bowl, mix together egg and cottage cheese. Layer in the crock pot as follows:

1. 1/3 ground raw turkey, broken up with fingers

2. 1/3 tomato mixture

3. 3 noodles

4. half of cottage cheese mixture, 1/2 of chopped onion & mushroom, 1/2 of spinach leaves

5. 1/3 of turkey

6. 1/3 of tomato mixture

7. 3 noodles

8. other half of cottage cheese mixture, other 1/2 of chopped onion & mushroom, other 1/2 of spinach leaves

9. last of ground turkey

10. last of tomato mixture

11. remaining 3 noodles

12. top with italian cheese blend

Cook on low for 6-8 hours, or high for 4-5 hours.

Clean Eating Crock Pot Chicken Tacos

Ingredients

- 2 lean chicken breasts

- 1 can of black beans, washed and drained

- 1 can of pinto beans, drained and washed

- 2 TBS of homemade Clean Eating Taco Seasoning mix

- Tostados. Check the label! Some are just corn and oil. Others are corn + flavorings + colors and dyes which obviously aren't clean.

- To accompany: Sauteed or raw veggies, Greek yogurt instead of sour cream, natural cheese, refried beans

Instructions

1. Add the beans, chicken and seasoning to your crock pot.

2. Add a cup of water

3. Cook on low for 5 hours.

4.
Open the pot and shred the chicken and stir it all together.

5.
Cook for another 15 minutes while you prep the other fixings!

Italian Style Meatballs

Ingredients

- 1 1/2 pounds lean, ground turkey

- 1 tablespoon garlic powder

- 1 tablespoon onion powder

- 1 tablespoon Italian Seasoning

- 1 1/2 cups clean tomato sauce

- 1/4 cup fresh, grated parmesan cheese

Directions

1.
In a large mixing bowl, knead the turkey together with the spices.

2.
Roll meat into 22, walnut sized meatballs, and place in a single layer in your slow cooker (Mine was a 5 quart).

3.
Pour the tomato sauce over the top, being sure to cover the meatballs well and evenly.

4.

Sprinkle the cheese across the top and set the slow cooker to low heat for 4 hours.

5.

Serve over pasta with a little extra parmesan cheese.

Quinoa with Vegetables

Author: Amanda Carlisle

Ingredients

- 1½ cups Quinoa
- 3 Cups Chicken or Vegetable Stock
- 1 small onion, chopped
- 1 tablespoon olive oil
- 1 medium sweet red pepper, chopped
- 1 small carrot, chopped
- 1 Cup Fresh Green Beans chopped
- 2 garlic cloves, minced
- 1 teaspoon fresh cilantro or basil (depending on your taste)
- ¼ teaspoon pepper

Directions

1. Rinse Quinoa

2. Dump it into the crock pot.

3. Add 1 tablespoon of olive oil to coat.

4. Stir in broth, veggies, pepper and garlic. Reserve cilantro for before serving.

5. Cover and cook on low for 4-6 hours, or on high for 2-4.

6. The quinoa is done when you can fluff it with a fork and it is tender. Liquid should be absorbed into quinoa.

7. Top with fresh cilantro and serve.

8. You can mix in garbanzo beans or black beans to add protein to this dish and turn it into a meal

Garlic Cauliflower Mashed Potatoes

- 1 head of cauliflower

- 3 cups water

- 4 large garlic cloves, peeled

- 1 tsp salt

- 1 bay leaf

- 1 Tbsp butter

- Milk (if needed)

- Salt and Pepper

Directions

1. Cut the cauliflower into florets and place in the slow cooker.

2. Add in the water, garlic cloves, salt and bay leaf.

3. Cover and cook on HIGH for 2-3 hours or on LOW for 4-6 hours.

4. Remove the garlic cloves and bay leaf. Drain the water.

5. Add in the butter and let it melt.

6. Use a potato masher to mash the cauliflower or if you want to use an immersion blender to make it more creamy you can do that. If it needs milk add it in a tablespoon at a time.

7. Salt and pepper to taste. Serve with chives or green onions.

Crock Pot Baked Potatoes

How To Make Crock Pot Baked Potatoes

Ingredients

1/4 cup extra-virgin olive oil

2 large sweet potatoes, peeled and diced into 1" cubes

2 cloves garlic, minced

1/4 cup coconut palm sugar

1/8 teaspoon red pepper flakes

1/2 teaspoon curry powder

1/4 teaspoon black pepper

1/4 teaspoon cinnamon

Directions

1. Add extra-virgin olive oil to the slow cooker and preheat to high will preparing potatoes and garlic. Add potatoes and all remaining ingredients to the slow cooker.
2. Cover and cook on high 2-3 hours or low 4-5 hours. We recommend using a 4-6 quart slow cooker.

Easy Chicken Stew

Makes 6 servings

Ingredients

- 4 x 4 oz chicken breasts, chopped into chunks (stove top method), left whole (slow cooker method) •could also use rotisserie chicken breasts
- 1/2 medium cauliflower, chopped into smaller florets
- 1 cup frozen corn
- 2 stalks celery, chopped
- 2 carrots, chopped
- 1 onion, chopped
- 2 garlic cloves, minced
- 1 cup jarred salsa (mild or hot, whatever your preference)
- 1 tsp cumin
- 1 tsp chili powder
- 2 1/2 cups low sodium chicken stock

Garnish: fresh chopped parsley

Directions

1. Place cauliflower, corn, carrot, celery, garlic and onion in slow cooker. Stir in salsa, place chicken on top and add broth. Cook on HIGH for 3-4 hours, or LOW for 4-5 hours. Shred chicken with 2 forks, place in bowls and garnish with fresh chopped parsley.

Tortellini Tuscan Stew

Ingredients

- 1 butternut squash

- 1 large zucchini

- 1 large yellow summer squash

- 1 large onion

- 1 large red bell pepper

- 4 oz. thin green beans

- 1 can crushed tomatoes

- 1 can chicken or vegetable broth

- 2 tbsp. fresh oregano

- 1½ tsp. chopped garlic

- ¾ tsp. salt

- 1 package fresh cheese tortellini

- 1 bag baby spinach

- 3 tbsp. Grated Parmesan cheese

Directions

1.
Combine all ingredients, except tortellini, spinach, and Parmesan cheese, in a 5-quart or larger slow cooker. Cover and cook on high 3 hours or low 6 hours.

2.
Uncover; turn slow cooker to high and stir in tortellini. Cover: continue to cook 15 minutes, or until pasta is almost tender.

3.
Uncover; gently stir in spinach and Parmesan. Cover; cook 5 minutes until spinach is cooked down and tortellini is tender.

Sweet Potato and Apple Soup

Ingredients

- ½ large onion, cut into large dice
- 1 lb white potatoes (2 small or 1 large), scrubbed clean and cut into 1 inch pieces with the skin left on
- 1½ lbs sweet potatoes (3 small or 2 large), scrubbed clean and cut into 1 inch pieces with the skin left on
- 2 apples, cut into 1 inch pieces with the skin left on
- 3 cloves garlic, crushed
- ½ teaspoon salt
- 4 cups chicken broth/stock (homemade recommended, can sub with vegetable broth/stock)
- 4 tablespoons butter, divided
- ¾ cup fresh sage leaves, cut into strips (using culinary scissors or a knife)

Instructions

1. In the bottom of a slow cooker put in the onion, potatoes, apples, garlic, and salt. Pour the chicken broth/stock (or vegetable broth/stock) over top.
2. Turn the slow cooker onto high and cook for 5 hours.
3. Puree the hot soup either in batches in a countertop blender or by just sticking a hand immersion blender right into your slow cooker (recommended).
4. Stir in 2 tablespoons of the butter.

5. In a medium sized pan over medium heat melt the other 2 tablespoons of butter. Add the sage leaves and cook while stirring until butter browns and leaves are crisp, about 1-2 minutes. Top soup with brown buttered sage and serve immediately.

Tip: Freeze leftover soup in individual servings for an easy lunch.

Slow-Cooker Chicken Tortilla Soup

Ingredients

- 1 pound shredded, cooked chicken 1 (15 ounce) can
- whole peeled tomatoes, mashed 1 (10 ounce) can e
- nchilada sauce 1 medium onion, chopped 1 (4 ounce) can
- chopped green chile peppers
- 2 cloves garlic,
- minced 2 cups water
- 1 teaspoon chili powder
- 1 teaspoon salt
- 1/4 teaspoon black pepper 1 bay leaf
- 1 (10 ounce) package frozen corn
- 1 tablespoon chopped cilantro
- 7 corn tortillas vegetable oil 1 (14.5 ounce) can
- chicken broth 1 teaspoon cumin

Directions

1. Place chicken, tomatoes, enchilada sauce, onion, green chiles, and garlic into a slow cooker.
2. Pour in water and chicken broth, and season with cumin, chili powder, salt, pepper, and bay leaf.
3. Stir in corn and cilantro.
4. Cover, and cook on Low setting for 6 to 8 hours or on High setting for 3 to 4 hours.

5. Preheat oven to 400 degrees F (200 degrees C)
6. Lightly brush both sides of tortillas with oil. Cut tortillas into strips, then spread on a baking sheet.
7. Bake in preheated oven until crisp, about 10 to 15 minutes. To serve, sprinkle tortilla strips over soup.

Skinny Tomato Parmesan Tomato Basil Sout

- 1 cup finely diced celery

- 1 cup finely diced onion

- 1 cup grated zucchini or grated carrots (or both)

- 2 (14 oz) cans diced tomatoes

- 1 bay leaf

- 1 tsp dried oregano

- 1 Tbsp dried basil

- 4 cups water

- 2 tsp Shirley J chicken bouillon or 4 tsp regular chicken bouillon granules (If you're vegetarian you can substitute vegetable broth in place of the water and bouillon)

- 1/4 cup butter

- 1/2 cup flour

- 1 cup Parmesan cheese, grated

- 1 cup warmed skim milk

- 1 tsp salt

- 1 tsp pepper

Directions

1. Place celery, onion, zucchini, tomatoes, bay leaf, oregano, basil, water and bouillon in slow cooker.
2. Cover and cook on LOW for 5-7 hours, or until vegetables are tender.
3. About 30 minutes before serving prepare a roux. Melt butter over low heat in a skillet and add in about half the flour.
4. Stir constantly with a whisk for 2-3 minutes. Slowly stir in 1 cup hot soup. Whisk and slowly add in the rest of the flour.
5. Add another 3 cups and stir until smooth. Add all back into the slow cooker
6. Stir and add the Parmesan cheese, warmed milk, salt and pepper. Add additional basil and oregano if needed (the slow cooker does a number on spices and they get bland over time, so don't be afraid to always season to taste at the end).
7. Cover and cook on LOW for another 30 minutes or so until ready to serve.

Black Bean Soup with Chipotle and Toasted Cumin Seed Crème Fraîche

Adapted from Bon Appetit

Ingredients

- 1 tablespoon olive oil
- 2 medium-size red onions, chopped
- 1 medium-size red bell pepper, chopped
- 1 medium-size green bell pepper, chopped
- 4 garlic cloves, minced
- 4 teaspoons ground cumin
- 1 16-ounce package dried black beans
- 1 tablespoon chopped chipotle chiles from a can (this gives it a solid kick, dial back if you are wary)
- 7 cups hot water (I just used very hot tap water)
- 2 tablespoons fresh lime juice
- 2 teaspoons coarse kosher salt
- 1/4 teaspoon ground black pepper

Directions

1. Heat olive oil in large skillet over medium-high heat.
2. Add onions and both bell peppers and sauté until beginning to brown, about eight minutes.
3. Add garlic and cumin; stir one minute.
4. Transfer mixture to 6-quart slow cooker.

5. Add beans and chipotles, then 7 cups hot water.
6. Cover and cook on high until beans are very tender, about 3 hours. [See note up top.]
7. Transfer two cups bean mixture to blender; puree until smooth.
8. Return puree to remaining soup in slow cooker. Stir in lime juice, salt, and pepper.
9. Adjust seasonings to taste; we found we needed more salt. Ladle soup into bowls.
10. Spoon dollop of toasted cumin seed cream (below) over each bowl and serve.

Toasted Cumin Seed Crème Fraîche

Hacked from Bobby Flay

Ingredients

- 1 tablespoon whole cumin seeds
- 1 cup crema or crème fraîche (or make your own crema, make your own crème fraîche, or swap sour cream or yogurt, for a close-enough taste)
- Salt and freshly ground pepper

Directions

1. Place the cumin in a small sauté pan over medium heat. Toast until lightly golden brown.
2. Place in spice grinder or mortar and pestle and grind until coarse. Stir it into the creme and season with salt and pepper, to taste.

Slow Cooker Turkey Chili Recipe

Ingredients

- 1 pound ground turkey breast

- 1 medium green bell pepper, chopped

- 1 medium red onion, chopped

- 1 Tbsp. canola oil

- 2 cans diced tomatoes (I like petite diced)

- 1 can kidney beans, drained and rinsed

- 1 can black beans, drained and rinsed

- 1 cup frozen corn kernels (optional)

- 2 Tbsp. chili powder

- 1 Tbsp. cumin powder

- 1 tsp. smoked paprika

- splash of Tobasco sauce (to taste)

- salt and black pepper to taste

- reduced-fat sour cream, cheese, diced green onions, tobasco sauce, and/or baked corn chips for serving

How to do it

1. Put the tomatoes, kidney beans, black beans, frozen corn kernels, and spices into the slow cooker.
2. In a large nonstick skillet, sautee the peppers and onions in the canola oil on medium heat.
3. When the onions are soft, add the ground turkey and continue to cook, breaking the turkey up into small chunks with a spatula or spoon. When the turkey is browned and cooked through, add the turkey, bell pepper, and onion mixture to the crock pot and stir to combine.
4. Cook the chili on high for 3-4 hours or on low for 8 hours. Season with salt, pepper, and Tobasco to your taste.
5. Serve the chili hot in bowls with cheese, sour cream, green onions, and corn chips (I used Garden of Eatin' Black Bean Chips) as you wish.

Slow Cooker Hearty Vegetable and Bean Soup

Ingredients

- 1 sweet onion, diced

- 2 cloves garlic, minced

- 1 medium sweet potato, peeled and cut into 1" cubes (optional, white or red potato)

- 2 carrots, peeled and sliced into 1" pieces

- 2 stalks celery, diced

- 1 cup whole kernel corn (optional)

- Kosher or sea salt to taste

- 1/2 teaspoon black pepper

- 1/8 teaspoon allspice

- 1 teaspoon paprika

- 1 bay leaf

- 1/2 teaspoon crushed red pepper flakes, more or less to taste (can be substituted with cayenne pepper)

- 2 cups frozen or fresh green beans

- 4 cups vegetable broth, low sodium (chicken broth can be substituted)

- ¼ cup freshly chopped parsley

- 1 (14.5 oz.) can diced tomatoes

- 2 cans cannellini beans, drained (navy, black, or pinto can be substituted)

Directions

1. Add all the above ingredients to the slow cooker, stir to combine, cover and cook on low 8-10 hours or until carrots are tender.

Tomato Basil Soup

Ingredients

- 3- 28-ounce cans whole peeled tomatoes
- 3 tablespoons olive oil
- 3 large carrots, peeled and finely diced
- 2 medium sweet onions, finely diced
- 4 cloves garlic, peeled and left whole
- 1 teaspoon crushed red pepper flakes
- 1 tablespoon salt
- 1 quart chicken broth
- 10 basil leaves (plus more for garnish)
- Freshly grated Parmesan or sour cream (for garnish, optional)

Instructions

1. Combine all ingredients in a slow cooker. Cover and cook on low for 5-7 hours, until flavors are blended and vegetables are soft.
2. Allow the soup to cool slightly. Then puree in batches in a blender until very smooth. Serve immediately, or transfer the soup back to the slow cooker and keep on low until your guests arrive.
3. Garnish with more fresh basil and some grated Parmesan cheese or even sour cream

Hearty Chicken Stew with Butternut Squash & Quinoa Recipe

Author: Dara Michalski | Cookin' Canuck

Ingredients

- 1½ lb. butternut squash, peeled, seeded & chopped into ½-inch pieces
- 3½ cups chicken broth
- 1½ lb. boneless, skinless chicken thighs
- 1 tbsp olive oil
- 1 medium yellow onion, finely chopped
- ½ tsp kosher salt
- 4 cloves garlic, minced
- 1½ tsp dried oregano
- 1 can (14 oz) petite diced tomatoes
- ⅔ cup uncooked quinoa
- ¾ cup pitted and quartered kalamata olives
- Freshly ground black pepper, to taste
- ¼ cup minced fresh flat-leaf parsley

Instructions

1. Steam the butternut squash until barely tender, about 10 minutes. Remove half of the squash pieces and set aside.

2. Steam the remaining squash until very tender, an additional 4 to 6 minutes. Mash this squash with the back of a fork. Set aside.
3. In a large saucepan set over medium-high heat, bring the chicken broth to a simmer.
4. Add chicken thighs, cover, and cook until chicken is cooked through, about 15 minutes.
5. Transfer the chicken thighs to a plate and allow to cool. Pour broth into a medium-sized bowl.
6. Return the saucepan to the stovetop and lower heat to medium. Add olive oil.
7. Add onion and cook, stirring occasionally, until onion is starting to turn brown, 8 to 10 minutes.
8. Add the salt, minced garlic and oregano. Cook, stirring, for 1 additional minute.
9. To the saucepan, add tomatoes, butternut squash pieces, mashed butternut squash. Stir to combine.
10. Stir in reserved chicken broth and quinoa. Bring to a simmer, cover and cook until the quinoa turns translucent, about 15 minutes.
11. Shred the chicken with your fingers or a fork.
12. Stir the chicken, olives and pepper into the stew and simmer, uncovered, to heat, about 5 minutes.
13. Stir in parsley and serve.

Soy Ginger Soup

Ingredients

- 1 pound skinless, boneless chicken thighs, cut into 1-inch pieces
- 1 cup coarsely shredded carrots
- 2 tablespoons dry sherry (optional)
- 1 tablespoon soy sauce
- 1 tablespoon rice vinegar
- 1 teaspoon grated fresh ginger or 1/2 teaspoon ground ginger
- 1/4 teaspoon pepper
- 3 14 ounce cans reduced-sodium chicken broth
- 1 cup water
- 2 ounces dried somen noodles
- 16 ounce package frozen snow pea pods, thawed
- Soy sauce

Directions

1. In a 3 1/2- to 6-quart slow cooker, combine chicken; carrots; sherry, if desired; 1 tablespoon soy sauce; vinegar; ginger; and pepper. Stir in broth and the water.
2. Cover; cook on high-heat setting for 2 to 3 hours. Stir in noodles and pea pods. Cover; cook for 3 minutes more.
3. To serve, ladle soup into bowls and serve with additional soy sauce.

Farmer's market vegetable soup

Ingredients

- 1/2 of a small rutabaga, peeled and chopped (2 cups)
- 2 large roma tomatoes, chopped
- 2 medium carrots or parsnips, chopped
- 1 large red-skinned potato, chopped
- 2 medium leeks, chopped
- 3 14 ounce can vegetable broth
- 1 teaspoon fennel seeds, crushed
- 1/2 teaspoon dried sage, crushed
- 1/2- 1/4 teaspoon pepper
- 1/2 cup dried bow-tie pasta
- 3 cups torn fresh spinach
- 1 recipe Garlic Toasts (see recipe, below; optional)
- Garlic Toast
- 8 1/2 inch slices baguette-style French bread
- 1 tablespoon garlic-infused olive oil
- 2 teaspoons grated Parmesan cheese

Directions

1. Combine rutabaga, tomatoes, carrots, potato, and leeks in a 3-1/2- or 4-quart slow cooker. Add vegetable broth, fennel seeds, sage, and pepper.
2. Cover and cook on low-heat setting for 8 to 9 hours or on high-heat setting for 4 to 4-1/2 hours.
3. Meanwhile, cook pasta according to package directions; drain. Stir cooked pasta and spinach into soup mixture. Ladle into bowls and serve with Garlic Toasts.
4. Garlic Toast
5. Preheat broiler. Brush both sides of bread slices with oil. Arrange on a baking sheet. Broil 3 to 4 inches from the heat for 1 minute. Turn; sprinkle with cheese. Broil for 1 to 2 minutes more or until light brown.

Slow Cooker Savory Superfood Soup

Ingredients

- 2 cups sliced carrots
- 1 large sweet potato, cut into 1/2" cubes
- 1 cup fresh or frozen green beans
- 1/2 cup fresh cilantro, chopped
- 1 small onion, diced
- 1 clove garlic, minced
- 2 (15 ounce) cans black beans, drained and rinsed
- 1/2 teaspoon crushed red pepper flakes
- 1/2 teaspoon black pepper
- 1 teaspoon chili powder
- 1 teaspoon cumin
- Kosher or sea salt to taste
- 2 cups vegetable juice (I used R.W. Knudsen, Organic Very Veggie Juice, no sugar added)
- 2 cups vegetable broth, low-sodium

Directions

1. Combine all ingredients in the slow cooker, cover and cook on low 6-8 hours, or until veggies are tender. Add a tablespoon of reduced fat cheddar cheese, if desired.
2. To make this even more of a Superfood Soup, add 2 cups coarsely chopped kale the last 5 minutes of cooking, or until wilted.

Slow Cooker Savory Superfood Soup

Ingredients

- 2 cups sliced carrots
- 1 large sweet potato, cut into 1/2" cubes 1 cup fresh or frozen green beans
- 1/2 cup fresh cilantro, chopped
- 1 small onion, diced
- 1 clove garlic, minced
- 2 (15 ounce) cans black beans, drained and rinsed
- 1/2 teaspoon crushed red pepper flakes
- 1/2 teaspoon black pepper
- 1 teaspoon chili powder
- 1 teaspoon cumin Kosher or sea salt to taste
- 2 cups vegetable juice
- 2 cups vegetable broth, low-sodium

Directions

1. Combine all ingredients in the slow cooker, cover and cook on low 6-8 hours, or until veggies are tender. Add a tablespoon of reduced fat cheddar cheese, if desired.

Chicken Noodle Soup

Ingredients:

- 1 1/2 pounds organic chicken pieces
- 3 cups water
- 3 cups chicken broth
- 1 teaspoon salt, or to taste, depending on saltiness of broth
- 1/4 teaspoon pepper
- 1 small onion chopped
- 2 carrots, chopped
- 2 stalks celery, chopped
- 3/4 cup organic mixed veggies
- 6 ounces noodles

Directions

1. Place all ingredients except noodles and mixed vegetables in the Crock Pot.
2. Cover and cook on low for 5 to 6 hours, or on high for about 3 hours.
3. Remove chicken from pot; take meat from bones, dice, and return to broth, and add the noodles and mixed vegetables.
4. Cook another hour or until noodles are done (about 1/2 hour on high). Or, cook the noodles separately and add them just before serving.

Vegetable and Chickpea Curry

Ingredients

- 3 cups cauliflower florets
- 1 15-ounce can chickpeas, rinsed and drained
- 1 cup loose-pack frozen cut green beans
- 1 cup sliced carrots
- 1/2 cup chopped onion
- 1 14-ounce can vegetable broth
- 2-3 teaspoons curry powder
- 1 14-ounce can light coconut milk
- 1/4 cup shredded fresh basil leaves

Directions

1. In a 3-1/2- or 4-quart slow cooker, combine cauliflower, chickpeas, green beans, carrots, and onion. Stir in broth and curry powder.
2. Cover and cook on low-heat setting for 5 to 6 hours or on high-heat setting for 2 1/2 to 3 hours.
3. Stir in coconut milk and shredded basil leaves. Spoon rice, if using, into bowls, and ladle curry over the top.

Slow Cooker Fudge

Ingredients

- 2-1/2 cups Chocolate Chips, [I used dark chocolate chips because of their health benefits. Ghirardelli is a good brand and works well with this recipe)

- 1/2 cup coconut milk, (canned, not in a carton)

- 1/4 cup coconut sugar, optional honey or maple syrup

- Dash of sea salt

- 2 tablespoons coconut oil

- 1 teaspoon pure vanilla extract

Directions

1. Fudge is perfect for the slow cooker because it doesn't scorch or burn.
2. Add chocolate chips, coconut milk, coconut sugar, salt, and coconut oil, stir to combine.
3. Next, cover and cook on low 2 hours without stirring. It's important that lid remain on during the 2 hours.
4. After 2 hours, turn the slow cooker off, uncover, and add vanilla.

5. IMPORTANT; Do not stir fudge mixture at this point. Allow to cool to room temperature, or it reaches 110 degrees with a candy thermometer.
6. Once cooled, use a large spoon, stir vigorously for 5-10 minutes until it loses some the gloss.
7. Lightly oil an 8"x8" square pan. Pour fudge into pan, cover and refrigerate 4 hours or until firm. This fudge is very rich and meant to be eaten on occasion as a treat.

Chicken Mole

Source: Everyday Foods

Ingredients

- 4 pounds organic chicken thighs, boneless, skinless
- sea salt
- 1 can (28 oz) whole tomatoes
- 1 medium yellow onion, roughly chopped
- 2 dried ancho chiles, stemmeds
- 1 large chipotle chile in adobo sauce
- 1/2 cup sliced almonds, toasted
- 1/4 cup raisins
- 3 ozs bittersweet or dark chocolate (dairy- and soy-free), chopped
- 3 garlic cloves, peeled and smasheds
- 3 Tbs extra virgin olive oil
- 3/4 tsp cumin

- 1/2 tsp cinnamon

- fresh cilantro, for serving optional

Preparation

1.
Season chicken with salt and place in a 5-6 quart slow cooker.

2.
In a blender, puree all remaining ingredients, except cilantro until smooth. Add tomato mixture to the slow cooker, cover, and cook on high until chicken is tender, about 4 hours on high (8 hours on low).

3.
Serve with rice and topped with cilantro.

Honey Glazed Chicken Thighs

Ingredients

1 teaspoon Kosher Salt

1 teaspoon Black Pepper

1 teaspoon Red Pepper Flakes

1 teaspoon Chili Powder

2 teaspoons Paprika

2 teaspoons Garlic Powder

½ cups Honey

2 tablespoons Apple Cider Vinegar

3 pounds Chicken, Thighs, Boneless/Skinless

Freezer Containers

2 Gallon Freezer Bags

Preparation

1.
Mix salt, pepper, red pepper flakes, chili powder, paprika and garlic powder together and set aside. Mix honey and cider vinegar and set aside. Un-tuck chicken thighs so they are flat.

2.
Cover both sides in seasoning and place chicken in slow cooker. Pour honey mixture over chicken.

3.

Cook on low for 6-8 hours or on high for 3-4 hours. If you are able to baste the chicken by spooning some of the liquid over the chicken periodically during the cooking time, please do.

4.

Take chicken out of slow cooker and let rest for a few minutes.

5.

Spoon excess glaze over chicken before serving.

www.ingramcontent.com/pod-product-compliance
Lightning Source LLC
Chambersburg PA
CBHW071821080526
44589CB00012B/880